An Ebony Cross

An Ebony Cross

Io Smith with Wendy Green

Foreword by Robert Runcie,
Archbishop of Canterbury

Marshall Pickering

Marshall Morgan and Scott
Marshall Pickering
34–42 Cleveland Street, London, W1P 5FB, U.K.

First published in 1989 by Marshall Morgan and Scott
Publications Ltd
Part of the Marshall Pickering Holdings Group

British Library Cataloguing in Publication Data
Smith, Io
  An ebony cross.
  1. Black persons. Christian life. Biographies
  I. Title II. Green, Wendy
  248.4

ISBN 0–551–01621–3

Text Set in Baskerville by Input Typesetting Ltd,
London SW19 8DR
Printed in Great Britain by
Cox & Wyman Ltd, Reading

CONTENTS

FOREWORD

It is easy for the institutionalised White Churches of this country to speak about recognition, reconciliation, and the receiving of gifts from the newer Black-Led Churches. It is not so easy to put this into practice. Io Smith's book will help us with this task. Above all else we need to understand each other's communal histories.

Io's story helps me to understand the background and contemporary attitudes of her Church and Community. I hope it will help others to do the same.

Robert Cantuar
Archbishop of Canterbury

In writing this book Pastor Io Smith puts all of us yet further in her debt. It makes another contribution to a major element in her ministry – the difficult art of building bridges between those otherwise separated.

For as long as I have known her, Pastor Io has set herself to understand other people and their ways and in turn helped them to understand her and her people in their ways.

Cheerfulness has always been characteristic, though I suspect it has covered more disappointment, frustration and pain than we would like to acknowledge. But with all her smiles Pastor Io has never ceased to ask the difficult question, to require a sensible answer and if the answer has been that a particular thing was impossible to enquire forcefully what could be impossible if it is the Lord's will! Her persistence in matters of faith, of social concern, of individual need has led her into all manner of strange company, archbishops and cardinals, local and national politicians and many more. In all these encounters she has been herself – to the great enrichment of us all.

Whoever reads this book will not only be introduced to a world of Christian faith and dedicated service which will be rewarding, but the reader will find a spirituality to deepen life and a vision to expand horizons.

I count it a privilege to have been invited to contribute this brief word.

(Rev. Dr) Philip Morgan
(Secretary, British Council of Churches)

One of the great challenges of our age is how human beings can live together with peace and justice. Within this general concern the specific concern for racial justice is proving of crucial importance. I have been privileged to work with Io Smith over the years in an equal and creative partnership. I believe that all of us, both black and white, have a responsibility both to be true to our own identities and to live in openness and love towards other people. I see the emergence and growth of the black Pentecostal Churches in Britain as a sign of hope and self determination and I pray and trust that as they exercise that self reliance so they may discover the blessings which come from being open-handed and open-hearted.

Tony Holden

ACKNOWLEDGEMENTS

I want to thank those Christians – of every tradition – who have given me their help and support in the work I do. I take this opportunity to specially thank active leaders of Christian communities, bishops and archbishops, members of the clergy and lay people. It is their tireless work and ministry which give light in the erstwhile dark places of the innercities. I believe, the results of effective praying are reflected through various projects, both secular and within a Christian context.

Special thanks to Pastor Violet Bailey, my co-worker in the ministry, for her relentless help.

In connection with the actual writing of this book, I am most grateful to Wendy Green for her patience and understanding. We held several sessions at her home and sometimes at mine, and it was more like fellowshipping. It was the first time I had shared the stories written here, especially those of my childhood and my early teenage years. I must confess that the next book I write will have to be when I am less busy. My day invariably begins at 7 a.m. and ends often later than midnight!

I thank all my family and friends for being so supportive, particularly my husband and children for being so patient with me.

Last, but not least of all, I thank you – all those who will take the time to read this book.

1

CHILDHOOD IN JAMAICA

I loved the time of my childhood. There were nine children in the family. Roy, Melvin, Ali, Alerick, Eugenie, Nerissa, Monica, and Ulla. I was the fifth. I was born on the 14th September 1939. As a result of a registrative error, the year of my birth was recorded as 1937, instead of 1939. I still go by that date officially though all my birthdays have been counted from 1939.

We all grew up in the little village of Aberdeen in the parish of St Elizabeth, Jamaica. My father was a religious man, a minister, and he grew sugar cane. He owned the farm, the land. We were almost upper class in the village. People looked up to him because he could provide seasonal employment. There were acres and acres of sugar cane and certain times of the year were reaping time. He would employ men to cut the cane, then the sugar was squeezed out by horses or mules drawing the mill and grinding it. We caught the liquor and put it in a big copper. Fire was piled up round till it crystallised. That was real sugar. Not refined. We used to put it in kerosene tins. They went off to the market on the back of donkeys and the sugar was sold so that we could buy groceries. Later trucks came and took the bundles of cane to the estate where there was a factory that made sugar and rum. It was the livelihood for most people in that area. When it was announced the cane was sold there would be a big payout. Everyone came. Wives and husbands and children. It was a lot of money. For most children it was a time for receiving new clothes and gifts.

I could not say my childhood days were ones in which we could go out shopping and buy the necessary thing every time the need arose. My father would take us shopping twice a year and we shared what we had the rest of the year. We would always be able to sell coffee and pimentoes and ginger on a small scale. We had all kinds of spices, especially nutmeg, cinnamon, and vanilla to sell too.

Father would work hard in the field, and he was a preacher as well, so the boys had to help him. They had to move the cattle, settle them down for the night, feed them and give them water. My father would come in from the fields and whatever fruit or vegetables he brought home he would divide the quantity and send us with portions to the neighbours, especially the older people in the village. In the morning he would milk the cow and the milk would be shared among the neighbours and friends. We didn't sell it. Most of the things we gave away. Lovely juicy mangoes. Lemons. There were so many lying underneath the trees, spoiled. People used to come to our house and collect fruit by the dozen, for free.

Everybody came to my father. Whatever their problem. If somebody died you could look out for a bearer coming to my father straightaway. He would build the coffin, direct the grave digging, commit the body. If somebody was going to get married or was sick they always came to my father. If a visitor came to the village and wanted some information they would be pointed to my father's house. The cricketers came. The politicians. The police called if they came to the village and wanted jelly coconut to drink. The poor ones came if they needed food for their children. They would always send their children at meal times and they would be fed.

If we were playing outside and it was meal time they didn't just call us in, they would call in all the children who were playing. Sometimes you would find fifteen or twenty children coming in to have a meal. I never ever saw food being cooked just for the family. People would pass my house and if they smelt the food was getting ready they would stop and join us.

At weekends my mother would bake cookies and that was a happy time for all of us as children. But she would get us up and send us away with cookies for this person and that person and we would see many of the cookies given away. It was not something we liked very much but we learnt that we had to share. I can remember being given a cake coming from school one evening. I shared it until there was just one piece left and then I gave it away. That brought tears to my eyes.

My mother never went out to work. Most women didn't. You came home from school to a meal and other children came home with you. All of the time I sensed my mother suffered in health. She would go some places, like going back to the village where she was born, but she wasn't an out and about woman. She did not participate in any outdoor life. She didn't go out to entertainment. She didn't even go to church. She was dedicated to her children and her home. I wouldn't say she was educated but she was a very sensible woman. She had

13

an intelligence about her. She didn't speak a lot and she wouldn't join in conversations if visitors were there, but she loved her friends, and people loved her because she was quiet and soft spoken. She never caned us like some mothers hit their children. She had an angelic spirit about her. She was the closest person to me at that time. If we were to be punished she wouldn't do it. She would say, 'I'll tell your father when he comes in.' You knew your father would punish you and you waited with your heart pulsing away, but half the time she never said a word to him. I loved her for that.

Neighbours, and people around could call on her for anything. If they didn't have sugar or milk for their children my mother would quickly share hers. We always had a big meal in the evening when we came home from school. Yams, potatoes, rice, meat, fish and lots of vegetables. All the children had to come to the table to eat. Many of the things were home grown. Spinach. Breadfruit. Corn. Bananas. We didn't have to go to the shops to buy them. We were healthy children. We never knew what it was to go to the doctor's, or take tablets. The meat market was in the village but my father kept goats, pigs, and chickens of his own. Fish, and other items we didn't have, came into the village with traders. The van came twice a week and everyone would dash out and get fish. Besides farming cane my grandparents were bakers. They would bake in a clay oven outside. Even roasting pigs or whatever was done on a fire outside because it was a village without electricity or gas.

Our house was a basic village house. All the walls were board. We each had our own rooms and there was one family room where we met for meals and to entertain

14

friends. We all had to put together to clean and shine the floors. We had to get down on our knees and shine them three times a week. When we were at school a lady would be paid to do it, but weekends we all had to help. We had to do the shopping, sweep up the garden, scrub the pots and pans, and cut flowers from the garden to decorate the house.

Every morning the boys would go off and tend to the cattle, and the girls would fetch water. We had running water, filtered from the river at different points, but we had to go and get it from the pipes, and make sure there was sufficient water in the drums for the day. We would carry it on our heads in pail pans, and had to make several trips. We had to see that the old people had fresh cold water for the day too. We would count and watch the time because we mustn't be late for school. Then on the last trip we bathed in the river. Maybe two dozen children. Boys and girls together. Splashing and swimming. We were so innocent. A single copy of the *Daily Gleaner*, our newspaper, would come to the man who ran the grocery shop. Every evening people would gather round while he read the news. Our first radio was a great excitement. All the people came to my house to listen. It looked like a box and we had to recharge the batteries every so often. We had some little Queen Victoria pans: little tin boxes like money boxes. We went round collecting halfpennies and farthings to send to the war that was being fought by Britain. In school we were taught Britain was the mother country. We had the impression that she ruled the world. The king was our king. Britain owned us, whether by purchasing us, or by adoption, there was some kind of relationship. We belonged to England. I can remember the bells ringing out the news that the war was over and the boys from our village who went to Britain to fight in the war were coming home. A dance was held out in the open air to welcome them home. Then when the king died people came out in the streets and mourned his death. We felt a part of England and we were proud of it.

There were many English people in Jamaica. The education was English. The teachers were English. The main shops were English. The governor was English. We were able to carry a British passport. White people came and settled and had servants. We looked up to them in those days in the Caribbean. Those who were really rich had a cook and a lady to do the washing, besides the people who worked on the farm. I knew of an English family in my own village, Mr and Mrs Earl. They had a daughter Margaret and a son Martin. We had to say 'Miss Margaret' and 'Master Martin'. They had big dogs and drove a little car, which nobody else could drive.

Most mothers would cook something early morning for the family to eat. About 8 a.m. Mother would call, 'You must come, get your chaklata, before you go to school.' Sometimes it would be porridge made from corn or green bananas. Everybody had their own cup. No one would drink out of my cup, and I wouldn't drink out of theirs.

We would carry a packed lunch to school with us if we were not having it provided. Sometimes Father would send someone to school riding on a donkey to bring lunch to us. He would make sure we didn't go without. If we didn't carry a packed lunch we would be given money. We liked that best. We could buy what we liked. We used to have ladies who came to school to sell things:

fried dumplings, fritters, coconut cakes, cookies and snowball. Snowball was ice that was crushed and had syrup poured on it. Every one of us wanted to buy snowball. If we could afford it we bought ice cream and mixed it with the snowball. It was heaven. We didn't have to buy fruits. Fruits hung over the wayside and we watched them getting ripe. Mangoes, oranges, tangerines, all kinds of citrus fruit and apples. We would gather it along the way to school. Even if it was in somebody else's yard we would pick it and run.

All the children walked in groups to school. It was a three mile walk. Six miles walking every day. That was something that kept the community together. Walking and talking and sharing. The roads were made up. They could take vehicles but they were not best roads. They were gravel. So for those children who couldn't afford shoes it was very uncomfortable, but because we were carefree we could walk and play along the way and it didn't seem like three miles. I remember clearly one young boy from my village wouldn't go to school unless he could walk with me.

Schooldays were a happy time for me. We were not among the unfortunate children who could not afford schooling. In those days school books and all the various materials were not free. My father provided us with the books we needed. There was no equipment like teachers use today. We learned by rote. Two times two. We had to recite poems, especially Shakespeare. Before I went to school I used to attend a little nursery in the village. I had to write 'proper writing' and when I went to school, the first time I wrote transcription on my slate the teacher took it and showed everyone in the school because it was so accurately done. I wasn't even five.

17

One of the most eminent sayings in my family was 'You must learn and achieve. You must be able to read and write. You must be able to try and pass exams and be professional.' School was a place we all enjoyed. We didn't hide away from school and play truant. In those days teachers gave us the cane if we were late, or fought, or were not attentive to our lesson. We had to learn. If we entered for an exam we had to put away our playtime and really study. We had to do our homework because if we didn't we would be caned. I respected it. I had to. If I didn't I would get it at home from my father. We had to be seen at the table doing our homework, even when we were only five years old. We would dress up in our uniform with our hair plaited and ribbons before secondary school. I used to do my younger sister's plaits. Sometimes we would do the plaits the night before, and tie them down so that it would be nice for the next morning. My mother was very good at plaiting and she would plait our hair in all different styles though it might take three to four hours to do.

My school uniform was brown and yellow. A brown dress with a yellow scarf. I can remember a special uniform when the Queen came to Jamaica. It was light blue with a white blouse. We were on parade and I saw the Queen very near. The whole island came out to meet her. They looked on her as someone special. We were taught to sing 'Rule Britannia' and the national anthem. Of course Jamaica flew the red, white and blue flag then and we all stood waving Union Jacks. At the coronation people were so excited. It was as if we were in England. We had souvenir spoons, cups, hats and skirts, and special celebrations for the schools right across the island.

I had a very good teacher for more than three or four years. Mavis was her name and she was from the family of Peart. She was like a village teacher. She sometimes rode a mule to school. One morning we were walking to school and she was ahead of us riding on this mule. Something suddenly darted across the road and the mule reared and threw her off. All of us gathered round her screaming, because as she lay there we could see that her leg was badly broken. There was a lot of blood. It was awful. Somebody had to put her in a car and rush her to the nearest doctor and from the doctor to hospital. I shall never forget that incident.

We had another teacher by the name of Miss Waugh who was a very attractive lady, well loved. My head teacher, Mr John Fraser, was very fatherly. Very clever. He had two children of his own. He wanted his students to pass exams, and he would see to it that they did their best. If we did not appear in school he would walk in the village to look for us. They were more than just teachers. They were like parents. Caring, loving and concerned.

I remember getting the cane only twice at school and once it was unfairly done. Somebody else was talking while the lessons were going on and teacher overheard it and turned round and whipped me. Then another time I went off to swim with some children and it was a dangerous place so when I got back to school I got the cane. My pride was hurt. I cried all day till the teacher came and gave me a pat on the shoulder. We had a few fights but we had to be careful because we would get the cane. In all my experience at school I remember fighting only once. I was set on by other children. 'Come on. Don't be a coward.' I didn't get the cane in school but when I got home I got a good hiding. My father would not tolerate us fighting at school.

We had to play out on the open field. It was a lot of land to play on but we had to create our own games. We would play cricket, volleyball, skipping, running races. Certain times of the year we had a sports competition. We had to enter into a test educationally and sports would be the climax. Once I won in running and jumping for my school. I never came less than first, second or third in all my exams. Then we were called up for a big prize at school presentation day. The parents would be there and the school would be packed. It was like a jamboree with lots of food and drink.

2

FAMILY AND COMMUNITY

At home we all had to participate in family worship, before breakfast in the morning and last thing at night. We had to read the Bible and pray. My father's philosophy was that a family that prayed together would always stay together. We were taught to thank God for food, our clothes, our shoes, our families. We would say the prayers that would affect us as we went out to school or play. Prayers teaching us to love each other and be kind throughout the day. In the evening we had to share the things that happened to us at school. If we got into a fight we had to tell the truth about what happened. We took it in turns to pray and read the scriptures. At five years old I was having to read from the scriptures and by the time I was six I could repeat passages by heart. From a tender age we knew we had to go to church because that was a way of life. We met aunties going to church and cousins and everybody we knew around us was in church on Sunday, showing off their best clothes, whatever. I liked to dress up and be part of that. We were part of the whole involvement of church life. The choir, the Sunday school. The minister knew our family. Everybody was friendly and it was lovely.

When we met them outside church they were somebody to us. They talked to us.

It was strict for us children growing up and we liked it. If we were late for a meal we had to give an explanation. We had to appear clean. We had to be respectful to people, even to one another in the family. We had to say brother Roy, or sister Jenny. We couldn't just say Jenny.

I was accustomed to strangers being entertained at home. One of our most frequent visitors was an Englishman, a Baptist minister, who had lived for many years in Jamaica and had settled there. He came frequently to my house for weekends and my mother would take care of him and cook his favourite meals. At Christmas there was always a houseful. It was not just for the family. My father would invite children from families that had no provision. We had to share whatever there was. Toys. Books. Meals. Clothes. We even had to share our beds. We had to let other children be happy with us. I was taught a poem before I went to school that summed it all up.

> *Let me live in a house by the side of a road,*
> *Where the tide of men go by,*
> *Men that are good, and men that are bad,*
> *As good and bad as I.*

That was how our house was. By the side of the road. Everybody came by. Some would come in for a cup of cold water when the sun was hot and they were thirsty. It all had to do with picturing a person to be humble and to be helpful, like my dad. He taught us to care for the old people in the village. We would have to see that

22

they got water and a meal even if they were not our relatives. We couldn't pass along the road without saying, 'Good morning cousin Jane. Good morning cousin Jack.'

The extended family played a very dominant role. Uncles, aunts, cousins. I only knew one of my grandfathers. My father's father died when we were babies. My mother's father was a very military man. He had something to do with the Queen's military service. He was from the tribe of the Maroons, the tribe that won the battle from the English in Jamaica. The English soldiers pursued the Maroons to a certain place but couldn't get any further into the forest because they dressed themselves like trees. So a treaty was signed. My grandfather was a colonel, the head of the Maroons for many, many years. I think once he even came to England to sign a treaty.

He had a very large house. We used to go there as children when school was on holiday. He adored his daughter, who married my father. He came once a year to the village to see us. He rode on a big tall horse and wore a khaki uniform with shiny buttons. He always carried lots of sweets and cookies and niceties for us. He used to tell me some lovely stories. If I ever complained he would say, 'Some people will never know when they are well off until they are badly off.' I've never forgotten that. It was special. He was interested for my father to give me over to him but my father wouldn't let go of any of his children.

His wife died when we were babies, but my father's mother lived to be a very old lady. Her name was Blanche. I remember her saying to me, 'Well my dear girl, I have got two silver bangles for you. I leave it in

23

the will when I die,' but by then I was in this country and I never got them. She said, 'When you go to England I want you to send me some money to buy myself a pipe.' She always smoked a pipe. She was a very strong old lady, strong in what she believed was right. She went to church but she could be miserable sometimes when it came to the fruit on her trees. We could not get to it as we liked. We must ask. She gave what she wanted to give you.

Whenever the rain was falling I went to her house. She had this large queen-sized bed with poles and a roof on top and lace curtains around, and lots of antique furniture. She would give us something to eat and we would go to bed and she would lie by the side of us until the rain stopped falling. From a very young age she used to tell me the slave stories. How when some of the slaves arrived they were already dead, and how they had to work and were beaten by the planters and weren't allowed to go into the churches. They had to worship in the cane fields. That's where they made their music and danced, because they weren't accepted in the churches.

'We comes from Africa,' she used to tell me. 'We weren't belonging here.' They were families that fought against the kind of colonialism that was enforced in the land. They were strong people – people who opposed the things they didn't want to befall their families.

As a child there was one thing I greatly disliked and rebelled against in my heart. White people came from England to Jamaica and had a black family working for them as servants yet they had to live in a separate dwelling. If the white mistress went to the market the black servant would do all the shopping and meet her

24

white missus at a point. The mistress would drive back with the grocery and the black servant would either have to walk or take a bus home. She wouldn't drive with her. I've seen that. From the day the white child was born you had to say 'Master King' or 'Miss Jane'. Whatever the name. Even with the minister's family.

In those days men took the leading role in all the activities. Women were not exposed as today. The men attended all the meetings and talked politics, and read the newspaper in the village. The women never went out so much. They were educated but they were kept behind. They had to be in the house and do the kitchen work. Father came in and his suit would be ready and the shoes would have to be shined. I used to grumble under my throat when Mother waited on Dad so diligently. 'Does my mother have to do all of that? Shine shoes? Dust the last little dust off my father's jacket? Watch till he goes from home, standing at the window till the last of him goes down the road?'

If he wanted a pair of socks my mother would have to find it. It would be, 'Where's my socks? Where's my shirt? Where's my tie?' I used to think, 'It isn't right.' That was one thing I was never going to do. I wasn't going to spoil my man.

3

TRAUMATIC TEENS

I loved the open free atmosphere of my childhood days. We could go to the river and swim. We could go out and play next door. We had open lands to play in, birds singing, and fruits hanging on the trees.

My childhood happiness came to an end when my mother died suddenly when I was twelve. I was a brilliant reader from the age of eight and I had been chosen to read the scripture for my mother that night. Psalm 94. She never went to bed without the Bible being read and Psalm 94 was something special for her. She loved it. Whether for strength I don't know. It was a sort of psalm of protection for her. She felt she could lean on the Lord after a hard day. If anything was bothering her she would feel that God was a God of justice and he would work it out. If somebody had offended her she would not fight back. She would leave it all to the Lord. One of her favourite verses was, 'The Lord is my defence, and my God is the rock of my refuge. And he shall bring upon them their own iniquity, and shall cut them off in their own wickedness.' (Psalm 94.22–23) She always went to bed at an early time of the evening, around nine o'clock. She died at six o'clock the next morning. She was in childbirth but it wasn't time. The baby died as well. The doctor and the nurse worked hard but they couldn't save her. The world was finished as far as I was concerned. I wanted to die too. It was a terrible shock. I had experienced my mother sharing the family meal with all the children who came to my home and the next day she was dead. That was the only time I saw my father weep.

For myself I would not unwind my grief. All the world went away from me. I locked up in my heart a bitterness against the death of my mother which I couldn't overcome. I questioned it. I thought my father didn't do enough to get specialist help. I felt that God had not treated us with justice. I couldn't understand why it had happened. My youngest sister was only two years old. There were four children younger than myself still living but Father coped very well. He was a conscientious father: very caring, very loving. He became a mother, father, nurse, everything it takes to see children through life at a tender age. It was strenuous to look after five small children. We had to be bathed morning and evening and given our meals at regular times. He was a good cook but we all had to join in. So I learnt to cook from a young age. He would rise at five in the morning and not go to bed until ten at night.

But mother care is something you can't compare. I remember the first Monday morning I went back to school after my mother died. Village people always stand about by the wayside chatting and I wasn't put together as my mother would have put us together to go to school. A woman criticised the dress I was wearing. She might have meant it in good spirit to put it right, but if my mother had been alive she wouldn't have had a chance to say that. She would make sure we were all right.

Shoes. Dress. Hair. Skin. All the right oil to put on our hair. I became very cut off and lonely. I just couldn't take the loss.

Six months after my mother died I went to secondary school in Kingston. I went to join my aunt, my mother's sister, and only went home in the holidays. I don't know if I enjoyed that part of it. My aunt was a very strict woman. She didn't have the caring part, and her husband wasn't a kind man, but I had relatives in Kingston I could always visit and I enjoyed my studies. I used to go to St. Michael's, a church school. We were inspected in the morning for tidiness and cleanliness. I had to have my nails polished properly and my socks had to be white, my shoes shining. I couldn't go there untidy or sweaty or with my blouse hanging out of my skirt.

I never had problems with my lessons at school. I was always a bright child and knew how to behave because of my upbringing at home. I was always a favourite of the teachers. I would sometimes go into school with a lovely mango and take it carefully to my teacher. The other children would say, 'She's Teacher's fancy girl.'

I used to do the teacher's errands. Once the master of the school sent me to the post office on his bicycle and in those days you had to license your bicycle. His didn't have a license and he said, 'Don't you ride the bicycle through the town. Just go to the post office and come back the way I sent you.' But I did ride it through the town, past the police station. I was hoping the master wouldn't see me, but he knew I was taking too much time and came out of school and saw me coming from the other end. 'All disobedience,' he said sternly, 'All disobedience will suffer.' I knew what he was talking about. I fell out with him for a while after that.

It was by then the reign of Bustamante. He fought with great conviction for independence in Jamaica. I wouldn't know all of the struggle but I knew him to be a patriotic man. He would always speak up for the rights of the island. Our welfare. In fact I was a great follower of Bustamante because my aunt and the family I was staying with were definitely Bustamante followers. I got involved with the youth group and followed Bustamante round the island. They used to write out these great big speeches for me to recite. I used to study them and lift up Bustamante. I was heading out to be political. My father was a follower of Manley, from the opposition. So when I was in Kingston I belonged to one political party and when I was in the country I belonged to another. I didn't know how to argue in those days.

My father was strict in bringing us up. In my home nine o'clock was bedtime. Even when we were teenagers. It was a disciplined home. We were not supposed to be out at ten or eleven o'clock unless we were with our parents or another adult. As a child I never saw cigarettes or alcohol at home. There was a rum bar in the village but it was not a custom to see women near there, especially in the bar. We had a dance hall. It was not very smart but people went on Fridays and Saturdays. We had to stay home and listen to the music. We couldn't go. Our father would give us a hiding.

One night I was tempted. Our father went to another village to preach on Sunday and he travelled overnight. There was going to be a dance in the village and I said, 'OK. I'm going to break the rule.' So when it came time for the dance to start I picked up my little basket as if I was going to shop, but I ended up waiting to have a dance. No sooner had I entered there somebody came and told me, 'Your father is around and looking for you.' He had come back for some reason. I had to dash home another way. I dodged and dodged and thanks to those friends I managed to get home and hide away.

As we reached the ages of eighteen to twenty-five we began to peel off from the home. Melvin left home to be a missionary. He went off to evangelise and became a preacher and pastor. Roy went off to the United States to seek employment with the farm workers. My eldest sister got married. I followed my education to writing first, second, third year Jamaica Examination Board and had a childhood sweetheart. His mother came from the same village as mine and they had both married men from Aberdeen. They had been very close friends.

My father was scout master and Len was a member of the scout group. Meetings were held at my home so Len would always be at our home at weekends. We walked together, ate together, played together. In the end we didn't realise we were falling in love. That caused a terrible upset in both our families. I don't know why. It's just a thing about some families. They know who they want for their son or daughter, and they didn't think I could cope with marriage and children at seventeen. It was resented a lot. We didn't understand what it was all about. Finally Len was sent off to Britain by his mother because the atmosphere was so tense. She thought this would finish the relationship between us. In fact this gave him the opportunity to work and pay for my air ticket to Britain unknown to our parents at home.

4

THE MOTHER COUNTRY?

In the 1950s many people were leaving Jamaica. The call was 'Come to Britain. The buses need you. The hospitals need you.' There were many, many areas of work that were advertised. The invitation extended to whoever would come. There were no immigration rules. There was no visa control. The invitation was wide that there were prospects in Britain. We were told, 'You can find a job. You can further your education.' We thought there was a better quality of life and a profession waiting for us. It was all a great adventure for young people like myself. Parents would sell whatever they could – their cattle, their land, and save to send their children. There was a hierarchy of acceptance for the people who studied in England and achieved, when they returned home.

I came because I was in love and I wanted to join Len. I wanted to finish my education and the invitation went out, 'Come to Britain.' I felt I was a part of Britain. It was the mother country. I came with a sense of belonging. I arrived from the Caribbean feeling as if I was coming back home. Even so it was very difficult to break from my relatives and brothers and sisters to come into a big country like Britain. It was like jumping in at the deep end, with no experience, and no knowledge.

I was shattered from the first day I arrived. I landed here and drove the route to Buckingham Palace. I couldn't believe it. It was nothing like the stories I was told at school about the most beautiful palace, or the pictures I had in my mind of England. People were walking the streets doing their own shopping. I thought they would all be rich and have large houses. We drove into the East End and I kept asking, 'I'm seeing all factories. When are we going to see the houses?' I thought with the chimneys standing up so tall the buildings were factories but when we got to where we were staying I realised they were houses. I had a bedsitter and I hated it. After shutting the door when I got in I felt as if the walls were caving in on me. I had always lived in an open house in Jamaica. The windows were open. When people got up in the morning the doors were opened. Six o'clock in the morning the birds were singing, the sun was shining through the trees, people were calling out, 'Good morning. How are you?' and stopping for a little chat. The village van was bringing in the bread, buns and cakes.

I missed the open life, the space, the fruit we used to go out and pick. Oranges. Grapefruit. Tangerines. Ripe bananas. Mangoes. They used to hang on the trees and ripen and nobody would take notice. The birds would eat them. Food wasn't something of paramount importance. You knew you had to have a cooked meal once or twice a day but we could evade that and take the fruit from the trees around.

One of the myths I found in England was that white people really believed that people who were black had been living in trees. I went into the doctor's surgery in the first month of my coming to Britain and this lady sat and looked at me and kept saying, 'Isn't it a shame. Isn't it a shame.' I didn't understand what she was talking about because I had only just landed and was not yet familiar with the way people spoke. When I switched on the television they talked so fast. Like lightning. Eventually the woman deliberately came over and said, 'Isn't it a shame to live in a tree?' My sense of humour was such that I could say to her, 'Yes it is a shame to go from limb to limb.'

It must have been the type of education that was given to most white people that they believed such things and could discriminate against someone who was black. Because my skin was dark one child said to her mother, 'Look at that lady. She hasn't had a wash.'

People talked as if we didn't live a normal life, we didn't have proper houses. When we walked into a shop everybody would turn around to look at us. If we began to speak straightaway they said, 'Pardon me.' I didn't know what all this 'Pardon me' was. Once I went into a shop to buy myself a bottle of vanilla. I was going to bake something and needed some nutmeg, some spices and a bottle of vanilla. The lady said 'Pardon me' about ten times, till I got very embarrassed. She called other people to come over to find what I wanted. Then I spelt it. 'V-A-N-I-L-L-A.' 'Oh,' she said, pronouncing it totally differently. 'Vinelle.'

Straightaway began a confrontation with the English language. There was a conflict between the English we were taught at school and what we were hearing in Britain. People didn't make themselves understand what was said to them. Their attitude was that I could not speak properly because I was black. In the West Indies we were a respected family. We grew up with a sense of being somebody. I was proud of my culture.

When I arrived in England I couldn't eat the food. In Jamaica we have the kind of potatoes grown here but they tasted so different. We can taste the real ground food in our potatoes. I couldn't stand lamb. Goat meat is more tender, has more flavour. My father used to breed goats so every so often a goat would be butchered at home. Especially if something special was happening. We never saw meat and things in windows in my village. We went straight to buy it when it was butchered.

I was not used to standing in a queue in the shops or at the bus stop. I had to accept the habit of drinking tea often because the weather was so cold and it helped to warm me. I couldn't stand gloves and socks and boots. Overcoats. Scarves. Cardigans. Thick jumpers. Warm hats. It was so depressing. The paraffin heater stank. It was even on our clothes when we went out into the streets. And the reception we got on the streets! The type of looks! There were not many black people around and when two or three found themselves in a market place people would actually stand still and turn around and stare. We felt as if we had landed from Mars or somewhere. We didn't understand what was going on. Back home we were part of the community. Here we felt totally strange. It was such a strain for those of us who came in the fifties. It was unbelievable.

People would meet me in the street and ask, 'What is the time?' They thought I only knew the time by the sun and since the sun had gone, October or November, or whenever it was, they asked me, 'What's the time?' I couldn't get accustomed to it. The ignorance of the whole thing. People even thought everyone here who was black was from Jamaica. I was asked questions like, 'Where in Jamaica is Africa?' They said we all looked alike. Everywhere I went they said, 'All black people look alike.'

I was bewildered by what I found and after the first few weeks my intention was to go back. I wanted to run away. I missed the closeness of my brothers and sisters. That was one of the most difficult things to struggle with when I left home. It broke my heart. I was a child in my own country. I could not get over the loss of the family closeness, the ties, the love and warmth of those around me, the community spirit.

Within five months of my landing in Britain Len and I were married. I owe him so much for making my life a success. He has always stood up with me. It was all a new life. To travel to a foreign land, gain experience, learn a profession. My expectation of Britain was that the streets were paved with gold. What I found when I came in 1957, especially on the streets of East London, was immorality, crime, racism, loneliness and depression.

Like many people who came across from the Caribbean I had no intention of staying in Britain for more than five years. Many, like myself, wanted to go back and suddenly found they could not. The money we earned was so little that by the time we had bought some warm clothes, paid the rent and had enough to travel to work we didn't have anything left. The whole idea of going home looked more impossible each year. I realised I was trapped.

Sometimes we would go out for a job and the first thing that would meet our eyes was a notice, 'Sorry. No coloureds.' I can remember going for a job and they just laughed at me and shut the window. I felt, 'If I was back home this would never be.' I used to do some teaching in the primary school before I left Jamaica. Here I couldn't work for anything which was worthwhile. I refused to go into nursing because I thought it was low paid and nurses were treated like slaves. I intended to go to school and finish my studies but I found that extremely difficult. Most places where I went for information the people in charge pretended I couldn't speak English and laughed and giggled and made a fool of me.

I tried all kinds of things. I went up to a clothing factory and said, 'I want a job to sew dresses.' I knew I couldn't but the man was very kind. He gave me a bundle of two, and those two dresses took me about two weeks to spoil. He gave me seven shillings for two weeks but I stayed there, and within six months I was making dresses for the model. Perfectly. Those were hard days in this country. I had to accept the system of clocking in when I went to work. I had to be on the job, and there was a foreman standing over me. He was just like a taskmaster pushing me. I couldn't afford to be absent even if I had a cold or was sick. The invitation had come out, 'Come to Britain.' They told us the jobs were here. I had clippings from newspapers. Hospitals, buses, railways. But when we came they were not ready to receive us. There were no proper houses, no accommodation, low paid work. My husband never really got a job that we could say was adequately paid and he had no choice but to work overtime. I felt I couldn't cope, but when we started having our own family we told ourselves we must cope.

Not only did I have to struggle with how I was going

to educate myself, I had to struggle to come to terms with the culture and the attitudes around me. I had to learn to cope with the prejudice, the rejection, the racism that was so very evident. We'd be shouted at, 'Go back.' We were called 'Wogs'. My face was slapped. I felt so rejected and unwanted. Back in the West Indies people held us in high esteem. I had status. I had freedom. I belonged. In Britain I began to lose all that. Each time I walked anywhere I would see racist slogans written on the walls. This began to open my eyes to the sort of thing Britain is guilty of, yet we had held Britain in such high esteem. We were told Britain was our mother country and mother is supposed to be caring, mother is supposed to be loving. But it was all different. That began to change my whole understanding of what these words really meant to people like myself.

I've been pushed off the bus, deliberately, by a white conductor. When I was at the head of the queue. I just stood there and cried. If I did get on a bus I could find I was the only black person there and suddenly someone would pick on me. I was scared because I was the only one and everyone pretended to be blind to these things. Black people would be spat at, shouted down, called names, have eggs thrown at them as they walked down the street. For many years I never felt freedom living in Britain. There was that amount of fear that something was going to happen. I was going to be attacked or something of that sort. All these things were very prevalent.

I took it at the time. I didn't know how to fight back. It is painful to bring out some of my experiences. They hurt. Had it not been for the power of forgiveness one would never be able to get over the feelings of bitterness.

Len is a different sort of person from me. He had insults thrown at him and all that. People he thought were friends called him 'Nigger.' But he didn't fight the battles I would fight. There were just one or two black people around and they couldn't fight back for themselves. Racism was not tackled in those days at all. Nobody cared. This destroyed the trust we had when we came to Britain. The attitudes of white people threw us off our innocent thinking. We lost confidence. Where there is no trust there can't be any good relationship. Where there is no confidence there can't be any love.

I want to thank God I had faith because in those days that was the only thing I could turn to. In my despair and loneliness I could always pray. The strength I needed I found through my faith in God. The Bible became more real, more comforting, more of a friend. For many people it was their only consolation. When I first arrived communities were all white. We were so isolated and many of our neighbours, even the people who lived next door, pretended that we weren't there. They said they could not understand us, or we looked like another person they met in the market. If we had more than three visitors they would call it a crowd and ask us in the street how many people lived in the house.

In those days we wouldn't see black people as clerks in the banks or the post offices. We never saw black people as cashiers in the local shops, in Woolworths or Marks and Spencer's. I used to make it my duty to go into Roman Road market because I would meet a couple of black people there. In the West Indies we didn't have to know people to talk to them. We'd get on the bus, and meet people, and start a conversation. Here people were rushing along, doing their own thing. There was no friendliness. If we could meet a few black people at least we would have someone to talk to.

5

WHY ARE THERE BLACK-LED CHURCHES?

When I first arrived I would walk into churches in East London and be met by a sea of white faces. There were few black people in the churches because when they had gone to be part of a congregation they had been turned away. The first place I visited was a church, but nobody said, 'Welcome.' Everybody stared at me as if I was some strange person from Mars or something. When the service was finished I didn't get a handshake. Nobody came out to me and said, 'Come again.'

A black person could go up to the door and stand there waiting to shake the minister's hand and the minister would hold on to the hand he already held for ages. They wouldn't even look to see, so we would just pass by. We felt a sense of rejection straightaway. One lady said to me, 'Did you hear what the minister said? He said, "Don't make your visit too often. It will scare my congregation away." ' Another minister told me, 'I think the church down the road wants black people.'

That disappointed me a lot. It made me sad. I was lonely. I missed home. I was depressed. I missed my friends and family. I was looking for love and warmth and encouragement. I believed the first place I would find that was in the church, but it wasn't there.

Christianity came to us from Britain but fellowship in the mainline churches was not possible. They had sent missionaries to the West Indies and pioneered Christianity and built churches. Like parents giving a child some sort of medicine, we had to take it. It was thrown at us. We accepted it. They were the people we looked to but when we arrived in Britain it was far different. Christians had been emigrating here since 1948, and earlier for those who fought in the world wars. They came with a faith. They had been working in the Church as leaders. They came as missionaries and pastors. They carried with them a vision and the burning desire of the faith of the Lord Jesus Christ which they practised in the West Indies. They came from various denominations, including Pentecostals. They naturally expected that coming into Britain with status they would continue to serve as ministers. The vision for the Church and for God's people was already in them, but it was difficult for them to build on the ministry they already had within a white church context.

Before we left Jamaica we were forewarned about the Christians who came to Britain and fell by the wayside. Even though I wasn't a committed Christian I had a strong faith and I believed in God. I knew all the prayers to pray and the scriptures to read in times of difficulty but had never fully committed my life. It was only tradition till I came to England. Conditions in this country drove me to the place where I wanted to pray more, and in praying I was drawn closer to God. I didn't just pray the prayers I was taught any more. I felt I really needed God because of the experiences I was having to handle. I needed a stronger force.

I went in the market one Saturday, not to shop but

41

to meet people, and one of the women invited me to a prayer meeting in a bedsit in a house near Roman Road. When people heard of a prayer meeting they wanted to get there. This one provided friendship and fellowship, communication and strength even though there were only three of us present.

When I first came I lived with a Pentecostal family and they took me to Dalston, to a church in Richmond Road. That's where I was married and came face to face with conversion. It began to burst open on me that I needed more than just going to church. I needed a change of heart. I began to realise that I could not fight racism with hate. I could not fight with a violence to hurt somebody. When my face was slapped I couldn't hit back.

That was just the dawn, the preparation of my destined contribution to the black-led churches in this country. There were not many black-led churches around in those days. We had to walk miles to the nearest one, or take a train or a bus. I think it was a divine timing for some of us to find prayer meetings in bedsitters, and black people who were really seeking to establish churches. Otherwise possibly my faith would be shattered, being turned away from places. It didn't shock me until I realised it was because of the colour of my skin, and the prejudice that was embedded in people. I couldn't imagine that church people didn't want to know us because we were black.

There were white people in Jamaica. White families with blue eyes. One of our closest neighbours was a white family. We wouldn't have known any difference if we'd put them alongside an English person. They were born in the village. One of them intermarried in my own family. The white minister was there also to preside over certain regions of the Baptist ministry and when he was going to be in the church in my village my mother would do the meal. He loved the way my mother used to cook rabbit. My father used to pile vegetables and fruit and all kinds of provisions on the donkey and we used to take it up to him. His wife used to be so very gentle and kind to us. So we expected the same treatment from white people when we came here. What I found in the British churches was rejection and unfriendliness. That's what made me change from being a Baptist to a Pentecostal.

In East London in the 1950s there was only one black-led church, in Holloway Road, and everyone who heard about it would travel to find it. There were times of real joy. Meeting together, singing, tambourine, music, rejoicing and hallelujahs. The way we know to worship. It was then I found what I needed. I found my ownership, my freedom, a spirit of belonging. When we arrived on Sundays some people never went home until after the service in the evening. Then I was invited to this little humble beginning of a prayer meeting in Clapton which Pastor Francis and his wife Julia started at their home. They invited me and I invited someone else. Within the Pentecostal prayer meeting there is a closeness. There is a way of freedom of approaching to God. We could weep before the Lord, and say to God how it was. We could do what we liked. Every time I went to that prayer meeting I felt I was strengthened. I felt more inspiration. I came closer to God. The memory of that feeling is dear to me and very valuable.

I continued with them and the number of people at the prayer meeting mushroomed. None the less it continued in the front room until Pastor Francis dreamed one night that he followed a road which came to a hall with a white man standing there. He shared the vision with us, and followed it up, and we ended up worshipping in St Barnabas' Church in Homerton High Street. We were put in the lowest little hall with all the broken-up furniture, dirty floors and no heat. We cleaned it up but sometimes they would have parties on Saturday nights and we would go in Sunday morning and there would be vomit and cigarette butts and everything. So we just cleaned up again and did not let it deter us from growing in numbers.

Getting involved with the black-led churches from a young age when I was bringing up my family has strengthened me. It's like a tiger in my tank. I would walk into church with my child and everybody there was so loving. Everybody wanted to give a helping hand. They took the child from me, fed it even. I just felt a belonging. Sometimes when service was finished I didn't know who had the child. They went from one hand to the other. They slept on one sister's lap, then another sister would take over.

Mothers in the black churches are so kind, so sympathetic, so tender in dealing with problems. Half of the story has not been told. It's not just going to church. A noisy bunch. It's that whole caring. To see somebody praying and preaching is outstanding but to see somebody taking my baby and holding it in their arms gave me a feeling of family. We might never have known each other. We might have been from different islands but that gave me the whole joy of loving one another.

All this was more than just preaching the gospel. They acted out the gospel they preached. This implanted something real in me. To love the Pentecostal church. If you are sick you will hear prayers for you from everybody. Visits will be made. People will be coming with flowers and with drinks. In this atmosphere of togetherness no one is better than the other. However simple you may be you are noted. I was a mother with young children but they would call on me to pray. They would call on me to read a scripture. When they saw I was a person who could do it well they helped to promote me.

Many would not know the quality of black people. They wouldn't know the affection and the emotions that we feel. In those days I don't think people thought we were humans. They didn't share with us to find out the qualities we have to offer. After feeling that emptiness and loneliness and sense of isolation all around me I began to pick up courage through the black-led churches, and feel that here was a community where I could belong. I felt a part of the family. I had found my own kith and kin. My mother had died when I was young. Those women in the church became as mothers to me. They were so gentle and affectionate. They took me as a daughter. They gave me the physical and mental support which I so missed coming from my own extended family. That was when I started to have hope.

6

BUILDING A FAMILY

Those days when my children were being born my husband took over the first two weeks of my coming home from hospital. After the ordeal of childbearing I had days of depression and feeling really low. Len helped to feed the baby. He changed its nappy and made it comfortable. While he nursed the child I had a chance to recover my strength and come back into the swing of things again. He has always been very supportive. I was able to do a part-time job and go on to college. I studied at night school while I was carrying the children. I achieved a few passes at O-level as the children got older in school, then I began to do secretarial and administrative work.

It was very difficult when I had to take the children to a nanny. I didn't want that. It was something totally wrong to my way of thinking. I only took two of the children to a nanny. I stayed home with the other four. I realised it was best to stay with my children in their early years. They develop better and the relationship between mother and child can be stronger. I breast-fed them up to nine months or a year. For eight years I didn't go out to work. When they were able to take themselves to school I started doing part-time work because we had to pay the mortgage on our own home.

Up until then we had been living in rented accommodation but it wasn't very good. The children have never lived in a council flat or high rise building. I made sure they never grew up in that sort of atmosphere but when we tried to buy our first home it was very difficult. We didn't get a low mortgage. It had to be paid up in five years. By the time we paid the mortgage and the bills we didn't have any money between us. Sometimes we had to walk to work and hardly had anything to eat by the end of the week. Just enough for the children. We experienced real poverty in this country. We didn't have money to spend on any luxuries. We couldn't even buy furniture. Len was working on the railway first and his wages were very low. He worked on the railway for years and then he changed to London Transport. I managed to get part-time office work. Accounts. Bought Sales ledger. I'm good at figures. I can do balancing and all that and I managed to earn a little money to help.

Many of the black families who made it in this country deserve credit. They came through a lot of terrible things to achieve what they have. Then one woman at work said to me, 'I don't hate black people because they are black. I hate them because they can come here and buy a house and buy cars. We don't have it so good.' She was definitely racist. She didn't want anything to do with anybody who was black. I said, 'What do you spend your money on?' She went abroad for holidays and she spent her money on furnishing her house. In those days we couldn't have a holiday. We didn't have enough money. So then she said, 'Well, we fought the war and you didn't have to, and now you're coming here to take these things away from us.'

Now this to me is unfair because the economy of this country is built by many other countries. There are many things this country doesn't produce. Tea. Coffee. Sugar. Rubber. Bananas. Cotton. Rice. We were taught about the economy in school. We had to write an essay once about how we were a part of it all. If stamps were sold in our country for three pence, two pence of that belonged to Britain. I suppose this goes on around the world. Other countries have helped to build the economy in Britain. We provided the raw materials and the cheap labour.

I tried to tell this woman but it was news to her. I think a lot of educating needs to go on to help people understand. Black men risked their lives to fight in the war. Many others never came back. But when it came to the honours, to marching up before the Queen, where were the black soldiers?

Some people didn't know how to cope with the presence of blackness. They had lived white for so long. One of my friends went to visit another friend who lived in an all-white street and when he left a neighbour said, 'I hope you're not selling your house to black people.'

Some of the mothers in the hospitals and clinics used to be so unkind. We couldn't let our children touch theirs. Even some of the nurses would talk about 'This lovely black baby'. That was so offensive. Why couldn't they just say, 'Lovely baby'? Once I went to clinic and stayed there from 9.30 till four o'clock. A nurse took the letter from me and said, 'I'll call you when the doctor comes.' Doctor arrived and everybody else went in. People who were coming hours after I arrived. Eventually I went up to the nurse to ask about my turn and she said something very rude. I turned away and came home weeping.

When my children were small I nearly had a nervous breakdown. I was never very healthy during pregnancy. Len was a tremendous help even though he was an only child. He did as a proper father should, sharing all the parental burdens. Feeding. Bathing. Washing. The children were never neglected. If he was cooking and I was doing something else I didn't rush out to take over from him. If I was cooking then he would bath the babies. We just shared all the tasks. Those days we couldn't afford a washing machine. He would go to the launderette, or if necessary wash, dry, iron, fold. If he didn't iron properly that was too bad. I wouldn't go criticising what he did. I didn't try to act the perfect wife, getting out the pans and baking to show off he'd married a wife that could bake. I said, 'We're going to bake our first cake together.' So we did and we spoiled it. But he couldn't blame me and I couldn't blame him. I was used to seeing my father doing everything, although in our country men are the ones to go out and women stay home in the kitchen. I did not like a lot of the attitudes relating to what is traditional in husband and wife relationships in Jamaica. I developed a resentment against them. My mother dusting my father's suit and cooling his soup and shining his shoes. He went out and my mother was at home all the while. Cooking, washing, ironing. That was not love. Love is a shared thing. Love is mutual. Husbands and wives should meet each other half way.

I've seen women after nine months of pregnancy still having to do all the work. Having children is quite a pressure. After giving birth to a child I think a woman's whole system needs relaxation and rest. I used to feel it was all very unfair. I promised myself that I would not structure my family like that. I feel when one member of the family is pressured it can cause depression, breakdown and crisis situations. Husbands and wives need to look after one another.

I didn't want Len to train me. I was trained already. So often people marry and they want to pick on everything in their partner that they feel is wrong and put it right. That's a wrong attitude. It is necessary to know one another as wife and husband and face the whole question of acceptance. As trivial as it may sound, most newly wed couples forget that they've never lived with that person before and that they have different ways. Invariably, when I have had to counsel couples experiencing difficulty in their marriage, the most common factor in the rift is that they do not want to accept each other for who they are. I was only just past eighteen when I married. Our parents opposed it but it's working! We've had quarrels. There's no such thing as a man and wife who never have rifts and misunderstandings, but it was something I didn't carry as a grudge in the relationship. Even if something was hurtful it was soon forgotten. There is something deep down in my heart for Len that I can't spite him. That must be a deep-seated love. I don't think I tell him very often but it's there in me. When we think about our rough patches it's nothing like some of the stories we've heard of other couples. Our troubles count as minor things.

I established the sort of love in the home which is mutual. It's not just mum struggling over the chores of a home to make a family grow up. It's family looking after mum as well. Then when they are old enough to be married and make their own families they will know how to share. At the age of eight my children knew how to get out of bed, wash, dress, and make their own breakfast before school. Not me jumping out of bed after working hard the night before, to lay out bowls for cornflakes, boil eggs, cook toast. From a young age they knew how to take on responsibility. Not sitting down waiting until a meal was cooked. Whoever arrived home first prepared the meal. I ensured that a hot meal was ready when they got home each day, that they had proper food, but I was not always the one who prepared it.

At the age of sixteen my daughters could prepare the Sunday dinner, do all the afters, make the trifle. Immaculately. If one cooked the next one cleared the table. It was nobody's special role to hoover the house or wash the dishes. It was group work. I fought against what I saw in the older families in the Caribbean. All of my children learned to be independent from the age of twelve. They were given their own linen basket to dump their socks or whatever there be. When the time came to wash they could go ahead and get their washing done. I never washed for them from the moment they had their twelfth birthday. If they didn't iron it properly or it didn't look right they just had to do it until they got it right.

There are three girls and three boys. Sheila, Yvonne, Jackie, Namshie, Glenton and David. Two of the boys became the responsibility of my father who took them and gave them proper schooling in Jamaica. As the years went by I began to mix in the schools. I had to see teachers and answer questions that were asked by my children. 'Why am I called black?' 'Why are we different from other children?' It used to upset Jackie a lot. From a tender age she used to come home and say, 'Mum, I'm not black.'

I said 'Yes. You are black. Why are you questioning me about that?' 'Because every time they keep calling me black at school and nigger and all those kinds of names.' So I said to her, 'You are black. Mummy's black. Daddy's black. David's black. Sheila. All the family. You've got to accept it.' I had to call her 'black Jackie' all the time until she accepted the fact that she was black. I told her, 'When you are called black don't fight. Tell them not to be jealous.'

Justice without violence is another thing. David used to fight at school when he was spat upon and called nig-nog and all that. The teacher wrote and complained that he was fighting so I called him and said, 'You're not supposed to fight at school.' He said, 'Mum – I know I'm not supposed to fight at school but they must stop calling me black and nigger and other names.'

I went to the school and said to the teacher, 'You've got to do something about it, because he fights when he's called names. You should have called the children who complained to you and ask them why, and scold them for calling him names. When you begin to do this then you will stop him fighting.'

David used to have a white friend at primary school. He would bring him home and they would have buttered rolls with jam, tea, fruit or whatever was going. This went on for months. But I didn't know that he couldn't go into his friend's house until one Saturday morning it was raining and he came home wet. I said, 'David, where were you?' He said outside the door of his friend's house. He wasn't allowed inside.

My daughter had a very close friend at school. A white girl. They shared classes and were both very bright. But one Saturday morning my daughter met her in the market with her parents and the other girl ignored her. She didn't say, 'hello'. She just took one glance then looked away. Those were some of the difficulties that the children experienced and they were not just things other people said. They were my own family's personal experiences.

By 1960 I was beginning to see more of a black presence in market places and shops, on the buses and trains, and that was encouraging, but we would see photographs advertising all over the place and never saw black people in them. My children would ask, 'Why are there no black people on the television?' They used to be questions that needed positive answers. 'Why this? Why that?' I lived through a lot of conflict. I was here during the Notting Hill riots. I saw fighting on the streets of East London, and on one occasion a black person running for his life from a group of white youngsters. I constantly feared for my children because of what I had experienced. It was from those early days that my concern for peace, justice and equality among people in this country was aroused. I realised something needed to be done about what I was experiencing living in Britain.

7

ORDINATION

When I first finished studying at college I decided to settle down in the church. I started working as a Sunday School teacher and did that to the best of my ability. Even though I was a young mother with four children of my own I made sure I was on time to collect my pupils and take them to Sunday School. I spent time over the week studying the lesson with my dictionary and my Bible. For a while I dedicated my whole life to that.

Then I began to act as secretary to the church. We didn't have our own building. We rented a hall. I would get there on a Sunday morning and sweep and get the hall clean before setting up the table and flowers and preparing the room for worship. We increased in numbers and I became very involved. Our pastor was a lovely caring man. He was a wonderful preacher but he didn't just want to preach to us. He gave us all the practical support we needed. He would visit us and encourage us to do something about the sub-standard housing conditions and was a great example. He recognised a ministry in me and continually encouraged me. After three or four years I took on the challenge and went to the London Bible College where I gained quite a few certificates and a diploma, which helped to deepen my Christian faith.

While I was at College I felt a need to concentrate on the work of the Holy Spirit to strengthen my Christian experience. Growing up in the BaptistChurch I had not heard a message or a sermon on the Holy Spirit. I had not heard preachers encourage the congregation to be filled with the Spirit or even to seek the anointing of God on their lives. It was strange when I entered the first Pentecostal worship service. Everyone was praying freely. The preachers were not preaching from notes, or out of a book, or telling stories. They just stood there with their Bibles, read one verse of Scripture, and without any notes were inspired to speak the word of God.

To me this was thrilling. I had never experienced worship in this form before. It was powerful. Those sermons moved me to tears. They were so emotional. They had life in them. I felt refreshed when I got home. I began to pray in earnest. 'I want this experience, Lord. I want to be filled with the Holy Spirit and to be led by him.'

It did not happen overnight. I had to be prepared to wait for this to take place in my life. I found it difficult to concentrate on studying for my exams and developing my Christian experience all at the same time. But now I have precious memories and am always willing to tell the story of how I prayed through and waited on the Lord, having fasted and set my heart to receive. I remember the first time I ever spoke in an unknown tongue. The same experience that is shared in Acts chapter 2 by the apostles. The Lord revealed himself to me in a new way, a new experience. It was something which was far beyond my own understanding, or my own ability. You can preach the word of God with your own intellectual, academic ability and that's great, but you can do more when you are doing it with the Spirit. Then when the word falls on a listening ear it gets down in the heart and makes a difference.

I was about twenty-four and had four children when I was ordained as an evangelist. I began to preach on Sundays and moderate the service. I felt a strength and a calling from God on my life. The older Christians would encourage me and say uplifting words.

'You are going to be a preacher.'

'You must carry on.'

'I can see that the Lord's hand is on you.'

These words were challenging. They made me feel that I was capable of achieving great things. It was very encouraging. When the pastor went to the United States he left me as the moderator. There were other people older than me, ordained ministers, brilliant scholars, but I was left to be in charge, with a certain amount of authority. I was doing evangelistic work, going to homes, and conducting Sunday worship and house meetings. I decided I didn't want to sit down in College and be the type of minister who walks around in gowns or ministerial attire. I wanted a down-to-earth ministry, caring for community. The inspiration came from my childhood experiences and from my minister. People were his concern. Caring for the whole man. All that was a pattern of the kind of ministry I wanted.

I realised that I had to be strong. I had to maintain what other people expected of me. The pastor was away but he would communicate with me occasionally. I realised that I could have been doing other things in secular organisations. The opportunities were there, but the Spirit of God told me again and again that there were people for me to go and help. I noticed every time I went to witness somebody would end up being a follower of the Lord Jesus Christ. Every time I taught the children they seemed to want to know more. If I prayed for somebody who was sick they would be healed. If I went into a broken home and ministered to that family they would be reunited. I could feel the Spirit of the Lord taking me in a leadership direction. As the years went by I could see the Lord using me for a direct ministry and I followed and prayed and dedicated my time and service to him. Eventually I was in charge of all the services, and had more and more responsibility.

Then I moved from Hackney to Leyton and during the move we lost the hall we were worshipping in. We had to conduct services in my house sometimes. There were about thirty of us. I knew I had an obligation to these people. They looked to me for leadership. I decided to look for a church or a hall, where we could get together for worship. We were only few in numbers and money was scarce but I was determined. I went out into the community and talked with people and began to look for a church.

One morning before I went into Leyton I prayed, 'Lord, I want to speak to three people when I get out there. People who will listen to the gospel. People who have a need to talk to somebody.' I didn't drive so I took my little basket and I went out. While I was walking down the road a lady came up to me, pushed her arm in mine and said, 'Isn't it a lovely day?'

Before I knew it we were talking intensely. The lady had recently lost her husband and within a few minutes the tears were pouring down her face. She had needed somebody to allay her fears of living on her own. Even though she was a total stranger I was able to encourage her and give her my own promise of being a friend.

Then I went into a shop and started talking to the man in the shop. He also unburdened his sorrows and told me that he had a broken marriage and was desperate. I began to tell him that I needed somewhere to establish a church; a building in which we could meet as a congregation. He sent me round the corner to the vicar who gave me information leading to the place we eventually bought and are worshipping in at present.

We tried to buy another larger building but someone else offered more money than we could. It was very difficult. There were no resources. We could hardly find somewhere to live, let alone to worship. It was quite usual to find small groups of black Christians conducting prayer meetings in a little room wherever they lived. Invariably they would grow in numbers until they could not continue in the bedsit. At the same time neighbours complained that too many people visited and the singing upset them. The times between 1954 and 1960 were troublesome days for the black-led churches. We were new and people were not accustomed to the jubilant singing. They thought we were a noisy gang.

Sometimes after many difficulties we would be allowed to use the hall within a white church building. Often it was full of broken furniture and the leftovers from the jumble sale. Some of the halls were used for discos on Saturday night and we had to go in on Sunday mornings to sweep up, clean and put things away before we were able to begin worship.

The kind of sharing that the churches gave us as black Christians was not sharing in reality. It was just tenant accommodation. We couldn't plan things as we wanted because they planned things too and we would clash with them. We didn't have an office. We didn't even have a place to store our things. Sometimes we went for service and there was no one to open the hall. They didn't give us a key. I don't call that sharing. We went through all those embarrassing moments where before the service came to its final prayer the lights would begin to be switched off. We would never be given use of the church itself. If we asked if we could conduct a special service in the church, because the hall was not really presentable or large enough, we would get a mountain of excuses. The Parochial Church Council did not agree. It would be too difficult. Et cetera. Et cetera. In some places today things have changed. Black ministers and their congregations can use church buildings. Sometimes they even share the key to the church itself, which is a real breakthrough. But in other places black churches are still not given use of white church buildings.

Black-led churches developed until some were able to tackle a mortgage and buy their own property. This was a tremendous advantage but meant fighting another battle. We were told time after time that the church authorities wanted the highest price for the buildings; or that the sale was not in the hands of the diocese or local vicar. The property would be given over to an agent and would therefore go on the open market. We would come up against ten bidders – commercial people – and we had to enter into the bid. We would start bidding at £70,000 and would end up at over £100,000. It was hard to get a mortgage. The banks would not lend us money so we had to go to finance companies who charged tremendously high interest rates. It is still very difficult for the black-led churches to own buildings because of the competition from commercial buyers. Ninety times out of a hundred when a building was purchased the heating system would be broken, the roof rotten, the pews in a terrible state. The congregation would have to spend an enormous amount of money to put it right before they could ever worship in it. Eventually the group I led managed to buy a prefabricated-looking building in Vicarage Road, Leyton and set up the church there. Then we could begin to lay a foundation for community work because we could not do that when we were renting a hall.

The black-led churches started in a time when many Christians who came here were lonely but were rejected from the central churches. Those who had a faith realised they had to continue in their faith. The black-led churches were somewhere for them to turn to, and they turned in numbers. As early as 1954 some of the pastors from the Caribbean were beginning to arrive here. That was the year the New Testament Church of God started. The organisation has developed into one of the largest black-led churches in Great Britain. In general these churches started from small meetings for prayer which developed into sizeable congregations. At this point a smaller group would break away from the main body and start another church elsewhere. Over the last fifteen years the black-led churches have divided many times. One might think that splitting churches is a bad thing but it has been good for us and has added to the growth. During the fifties, sixties and up to the seventies churches were springing up all over the communities in Britain. Because of the sort of depression and oppression that surrounded immigrants in this country they needed something to lift their spirits. They needed to hear good news. They needed to know that there was hope.

Some of the pastors of the black-led churches are willing, not only to go in the pulpit and preach, but also to serve the community. They will drive the van or their car to collect people for service. They help in spiritual matters and everyday concerns. They will go to hospitals, visit prisons. They do this because they believe that the gospel cares for the whole man. We cannot preach the gospel to someone who is hungry and expect a positive response unless we feed them physically.

This attitude is part of the process of the growth of the black-led churches. We see evangelism as everybody's responsibility. Not just the task of someone who has graduated from Cambridge or Oxford University. Whether they be brother, sister, pastor, bishop they share the gospel with other people and the church grows. It's so simple. It's just a matter of finding people where they are. People are always searching. There's always somebody in the community who wants to hear the gospel. It doesn't matter how many reject it. Somebody's always there that has a need fulfilled.

We take the gospel to the high rise flats. We share it at work. Even on the bus sometimes though people think we are a nuisance. When we sing and are cheerful at work people ask, 'What do you have to sing, or smile about?' To black Pentecostal Christians the whole concept of finding Christ and the love, joy, and peace that he brings is sharing the good news. The way the black person feels joyful and cries, that's how the white person feels. We are made of the same flesh and blood. In the image of God. We share humanity. This is why I believe there should be equality among people.

The word black-led is not meant as a mark of separation. After careful consideration on the part of black ministers, we decided to identify our churches as blackled. It does not mean that only black people go to these churches. It simply means that we are identified under the leadership which is black. There are a mixture of ethnic minorities within the black-led churches, as well as members who are not black people. But the name serves to identify an indigenous leadership within its own context. It does not mean that God has a white church and a black church in Britain. We are all identified with the one kingdom. The Church is all of God's people.

The black-led churches were attacked for being noisy in the early days because it was not something the community was accustomed to from a church. In the West Indies people sang, shouted, and played musical instruments, making a wonderful noise to the Lord. This was natural to the people living near the church. They recognised it was part of the whole worshp and praise. There was no complaint. In Britain it stood out because it was something new. I remember when we first arrived in Vicarage Road there were complaints from the neighbours and we expected a police officer to arrive at worship times. Petitions were signed. The building itself was attacked. Windows were smashed. People came in even during services to say we were making too much noise. I assured the community that we were there to stay. The church had been quiet and dead for a number of years. Now it was coming alive. The worship was jubilant and anyone was free to come and join us and have a good time.

8

MINISTERING AS A WOMAN

The ministry was something I wanted to do, and I held it dearer than anything else in my whole life. To be a minister of God. To be a pastor. Some men have said to me, 'I don't mind you being a minister, but not a pastor.' I didn't find hostility from my first leader. He was of a different character. But I have had problems with some men I have worked with since.

I can think of times when I had to conduct marriages and funerals and men came along in wonder. They were shocked to find a woman officiating. At the end of the service they would come and tell me, 'Well I haven't got any criticism. It was accurately done.' As if to say they were surprised because they had expected mistakes to be made and that I would do it less well than a man.

When I speak about the pastoral ministry I am not just talking about counselling and teaching, but about women being ordained and given full authority to carry out leadership of a congregation. In my own denomination we have many ordained women leading lively, successful congregations. Some black-led churches are still against women being pastors, but in the New Testament Assembly there is a freedom to develop in ministry, for women as well as men. In the New Testament

Assembly women lead most of the praise and worship which is the liveliest part of the service. They are also very effective at bringing out the church in intercessory prayer. These are very substantial and important ministries within the congregation of God's people.

In the New Testament Assembly there is opportunity to share in all the activities of the church and to participate in any ministry for young, old, male, female, ordained or not. Quite a number of young people in our churches are involved in preaching, moderating the services, sharing in the worship and providing the music and singing. They feel they belong to whatever is going on and it gives them joy in being part of it.

In other church movements a woman can only participate to a small extent though there are still some black-led churches which do not ordain women as pastors. They can be evangelists and missionaries but not pastors. In some churches they are not used to serve communion. For many years I worked quietly 'within my place'. This is a term men in the church use to refer to women. It hurt but I was not bold enough to challenge it. I went through a lot but it didn't put me down. It made me tough. There was always conflict about the role of women in the church then. It continued while the church grew in numbers until I moved from Hackney to Leyton. Then when I began to function as a minister I found resentment from other ministers. I remember a bishop looked at me as if to say, 'What on earth do you think you're doing?' when I turned up at this Anglican church to preach.

There were countless incidents where I would be talked down to, and would sit around having to listen to men discussing how Paul said women should be kept silent in the church. Their interpretation was always that you shouldn't be in the ministry if you were a woman. It was a real struggle. I knew that women needed a voice, especially in the church when it came to being ordained and taking up their rightful position as full ministers. But sometimes I was very, very timid in speaking up because I didn't want to give the impression that I was vindicating myself. I didn't want to say anything, yet at the same time I knew I had to speak. I wanted to say, 'It's not right. God did not mean it like this.' It was there inside me. It hurt. I wanted to explode at times.

I came up against male domination from the time I entered the church, even when I was ordained in my own right as a minister. I began to ask myself many questions. 'If I'm ordained and have been given a ministerial certificate, how is it my role in the church seems to be different to that of the men?' All the ordinances were male dominated; the serving of the Lord's supper, the christening of babies, the marriages, funerals, baptisms. Even the simplest things to do with the service were all done by men.

I began to question ordination and what it meant and to look more closely at when Jesus ministered to women. I started to realise that through the Scriptures God used women to cement his divine plan. Ruth. Naomi. Esther. Deborah. God knew he could depend on these women to be faithful, to be honest, to listen to what he was saying to them. There couldn't have been a Saviour unless God had come down in Mary. Where the scripture says, 'In the kingdom of God there is neither male nor female' it's a fact. God would never bring his creation together without women's ministry.

People argue women were not apostles and all that, yet they were last at the cross and first at the tomb. They heard Jesus crying out to his Father when he gave up the ghost. They had him on their hearts. They loved him in life. They loved him in death. They were the first ones to find the tomb and discover the resurrection. So often this has been preached around by men. They saw the cross. They saw Peter. They saw the tomb and the angel . . . but they never saw what the women did; that they were bold and brave. They did not question who would roll away the stone. They just made their way to the tomb. Stories like this have rarely been preached about. Men avoid them.

Paul came down strong upon women because they were beginning to fight back but even he commended them and reminded the early church not to forget the women who laboured with them and were succourers. Women do succour the church. When a woman is pastoring an assembly she is as close to the flock as to the child on her breast. They have a tender feeling towards someone in their struggle and will give out to them as if they are breast-feeding a child. They watch their growth closely. Sometimes I have only to sit and listen to someone crying to know exactly what is coming behind that feeling. I'm not saying a man might not do that but I am saying a woman can be equally successful in carrying out pastoral ministry.

Women must not feel guilty because men are so hostile. I'm sure Mary had a lot of trouble when she was pregnant. Can you imagine the hostility in that kind of culture? A Jewish girl pregnant without marriage? We have to be in solidarity with Mary sometimes and stand

67

up. I don't know why men leave these things out of their theology.

I find that being a woman has helped me considerably in my ministry. In some cases men preach as if God is a big daddy who comes to their defence at all times and who fights every battle. I see God as a loving mother with a tender touch, who cares, who understands, who is affectionate, wise. I preach God as a saviour, as a friend, and as a mother. Many people do not bring out the true motherhood of God, or see God as one who cares, who picks you up when you fall. Just like a mother when the child falls over. She picks it up and kisses the bruise and soothes it.

I think it is language that has given God a masculine image, made God a man. The writers of the Bible have put masculine gender all the time on scripture. He and him. Father and so forth. If we look more closely at the nature of God it is possible to see more of a mother/ father caring situation. We should not put a sex on God when we look at the Scriptures and see how God behaves and acts. The scripture says that God is spirit therefore we should not put a sex title on spirit. We cannot define a man's spirit from a woman's spirit. God should not be seen as man and then used to discriminate against women.

When a woman is debarred from the ministry it is hindering God's work and the progress of that caring motherhood in the church. I think of the irony of some of the things men have said about women's ministry. There's a lot that men and women could teach each other. Being a woman I am able to touch the sensitive areas of families. There are some things a family will sit down and discuss with me they won't tell a man. We have that motherly touch in giving advice and dealing with these issues. This doesn't mean that women minister in these terms only to women. We should also minister to men in that soft, gentle manner. Pastoral ministry is something I have learned. I've learnt how to care, how to be responsible, how to share people's frustrations and suffering. There is a parallel between the role of mother and being a female minister. Cleaning up the home. Bathing the children. Preparing a meal. Spiritually it's very similar. I don't see my ministry as an elevated role. I see it as servanthood. Being a woman in the ministry has its value. There is a unique closeness to the community, to the congregation.

I have heard men say, 'No way would God use a woman.' That makes some women feel as if they're doing the wrong thing. I would advise women who sense the call of God to the ministry to count this a great honour. Go forward. Do not even stop to worry about what men think. You are not changing your womanhood in being able to stand up with the men. You can be a prosperous and progressive minister as a woman and you don't have to be masculine. You can use your charm, and your motherhood, and your experience as a female. You don't have to dress like the man, talk like the man, or behave like the man. You can have your own style of ministry which God can use in a very successful way. The more successes you have the more you grow into your confidence. When God is with you, then the whole world is with you.

What women really need to be concerned about is their assurance of the call of God to the ministry. If men cannot accept women because of their womanhood they will have to accept them for the work they do. Women should not be put off because they are not accepted. Jesus too suffered rejection. Never feel challenged. If women begin to feel challenged then they are going to become competitive. Once they begin to compete they will lose sight of what God wants them to do. I know where there is a strong woman, an able and capable woman, men always feel threatened. Carry on with what you can do. Feel happy and relaxed and confident that God is using you as a minister and remain like that. It is difficult to work in a dominantly male setting. Sometimes you may be the only woman working in that situation. Or you may have other women but their awareness is not awakened. They just feel happy and satisfied with the system. I'm not happy in that situation so I rebel. In secular society women are gaining degrees and higher status. They are taking their rightful positions. That is a challenge for me. I do not accept some of the things set up around me. I would rebel against the system and try to change it. It takes a long time and involves conflict but I am aware that without conflict there can't be any change. The woman has got to be prepared to be bold, to be the voice, to be courageous. So there are some very painful experiences working across the whole frontier of the various systems.

9

CONTRASTING CULTURES

For thirteen years I had not gone back to see my father or my brothers and sisters in Jamaica. All those years when I was building a family and struggling to set up home properly I knew I couldn't go home. I had to be here. Then when the children reached a certain age I had the privilege to go back. That was a glorious time, especially as I managed to go back as a preacher. The Baptist Church opened the doors and all the churches in the village. I ran a lot of crusades while I was there and many, many people accepted the Lord Jesus Christ and were baptised.

Then I knew that the Lord was calling me back to the evangelistic ministry. Not just in Britain. More and more doors began to open. I began to go to other islands in the Caribbean and when I went to the United States to see friends and relatives, doors opened there and the result was great. I've always wanted to travel to Africa to preach the gospel and I've been there four times now to minister, counsel and teach the Christians in the villages. Now there is a school in Ghana with three hundred children.

There was a time when I gave up all my paid jobs for the ministry but it's something about me that I have to be able to keep my independence. I don't want to let go of that. Going out to work gives me the chance to meet new people and get experience of what's going on in the outside world. It is a whole part of what I want to do, even if it's part-time. I've been asked many times how do I fulfil the role of minister and look after my family. The answer to that is, 'We look after one another.'

I admit I could sometimes hurt them by their not seeing me. I remember once when I was going away on a mission Jacqueline threw herself down on the floor and screamed. She was about ten or eleven and very attached to me. That broke my heart, so I tried to do something about it. She'd never reacted before but it was possibly inside. Sometimes we had family forums and I'd ask them, 'What is it about me you want to change?'

It's good to talk. You should talk. Even if the worst thing is going to come out. Jacqueline said she didn't like it when I fasted. I used to fast for days. She thought I would be hurt and die. She never liked it when I went on an aeroplane flight. And she didn't like me being a pastor because I was a target to people. When people talked about me as the pastor she felt hurt. I had to sit her down and explain that these things had to be because it's the way that my life has been ordered. It's the things that make me happy. That I want to do. When she comes of age to choose whatever makes her happy that's what I have to accept. It's the whole acceptance of who people are.

My father was strict in bringing us up but today I can look back and thank him for the security I enjoyed as a child. Childhood meant a stable foundation, both religious and social, with the extended family and neighbours all around me. There was no time for barriers. No time for the question of who was better than who. We all shared in the same meals. We went to school together. We swam together in the same pools. We never knew selfishness or to put people in categories.

These things meant something to me and remained fresh in my mind. They were helping me to realise that all human beings are created alike. The whole episode of my childhood caused me to plunge into a lot of things when I faced them in this country. My childhood upbringing has to do with what I am today. I can appreciate my childhood days now that I have grown and travelled and seen the world; different communities, other children growing up with parents. This is why I believe children should appreciate their parents. A mother's touch is something meaningful. Fixing the hair, choosing lovely outfits, dressing up. I have not departed from all my religious upbringing. When you have to bring up your own children it's a good help. A foundation. I know children today don't like the thought of the strict discipline. Society has changed. In big cities and towns teenagers are free to be on the street at 3 o'clock in the morning. It's a totally different environment, a totally different upbringing and a totally different culture. It was very difficult when I began to grow my own children. I have not inflicted on them some of the rules I had to abide by when I was young because of the difference in culture in this country.

I would love to see grown-up children today having to accept some of the rules I had to accept as a child. Even at the age of thirteen we had to go to bed at nine o'clock and make sure we got our homework over at a good time in the evening. I have to admire my father. Of all the brothers and sisters at home I can look back over the years and say that we have not once got in trouble with the police or had to be reprimanded or anything like that. We did not have everything other children had, but we had a life of happiness together. The feeling I experienced then I have not felt in all my years living in this country. I wish I was able to give my own children the sort of childhood I had. All of us didn't attain to the heights that were set for us but some of us were fairly able to be professional. When my brothers and sisters have a chance of meeting the first thing we talk about are our childhood days. They gave us strength to live in whatever circumstances we find ourselves in London, New York, or other big cities where there is no sort of community spirit around. The whole foundation in the faith which was embedded in us as children helps us to overcome stress and the pressures of life.

I'm often told by my own children that those days people were not educated and so forth, but they were good days. We were told what to do and we did what we were told. We never cheated our parents or told them words which should not have been said, or talked up to them in a disobedient manner. I appreciated those days as a child and they gave me direction for bringing up my own children. A lot of my upbringing has rubbed off on them, but they just naturally turned their own way when they reached a certain age. I didn't have problems with them stealing or getting into trouble with the police or having to go to remand homes to visit any of them. Nothing of that sort. But I had growing fears for them on the street, especially as my children were teenagers when the whole SUS law came up. They were so vulnerable.

One evening my son left home with a friend and at about three o'clock in the morning the telephone rang. It was the police. They had picked up my son and his friend and taken them to the police station. They said they were driving a stolen car. It was far beyond the truth but the police didn't want to listen to their story properly. Thank God they were not charged.

Those of us who have youngsters growing up in this country live with fear. Society is not a safe place. It's always the worst stories that are picked up and give the wrong impression of black people. I want society to understand that not every black youngster that walks out onto the streets of England is a mugger. I know a young man who came to this country. He was born here but he left the country at the age of six and went back to the Caribbean with his parents. He's grown now and realises he's British and wants to rejoin his family. I was the one who was asked to receive him. About two weeks after he came here he was walking up the street and this lady was coming towards him. She started to hide away her handbag and look at him strangely as if he was going to snatch her bag. He was so embarrassed. He came up to me and said, 'Is this the way it is in Britain? Does everyone look on you as a mugger?' It's the way black people are stereotyped.

There is a lot more work to be done to build the confidence of the black community regarding the police. The black community has lost the trust that they had during the early days of coming to this country. Today there are growing tensions between the black community and the police, especially among the younger generation.

This is a sensitive area that needs a great deal of work to be done from both sides.

A lot of morals have been lost in this country from families that have grown up in the Caribbean. Parents set up a standard in the home but society breaks it down. In fact society's saying to Christian families, 'Open the gate' and we are suffering for it. Our children are turning to drugs and all sorts. The permissiveness has affected good living in this country. Christian values are not taken on board and dealt with seriously. When we try to put down strictness in the family the children are laughed at and told they are stupid by their friends. Up to the time when my daughters were eighteen and twenty years of age I would know where they were off to and they would phone home if they were coming in later than ten o'clock. That sounds old-fashioned but I think it's a battle between what the masses say and what Christian values/ethics are to homes in this country. Even though my own children have passed through that now and have turned their own way they still have faith, recognise Christian values and respect the work I am doing.

I had an incorrect concept of Britain as a Christian country. It's sad but I don't know how many realise that the faith is slipping from under the feet of people. I don't know what else is going to bring the nation back. When I make visits to prisons and places like that it concerns me to see so many valuable people behind bars or in mental hospitals. I cannot sit down and blame the state for them being there. I blame it on unemployment and the pressures of society. I have got to send out a message clear and plain to the parents. Whatever we can do to help and support our youngsters, do it. The situation is not getting any better. Give your child the support from day one in school and so forth.

I know there are some children who are causing a lot of concern. There are pathetic cases where the children are convicts from a tender age. I do not believe putting young people in prison is the way to help. I would want to see more centres where parental care is offered for these children who have gone wayward. When you put some of these youngsters into prison they get worse and when they leave the after-care is not sufficient. We cannot provide the type of services needed because we haven't got the money to do it. We haven't got the facilities. We haven't got the buildings to set up the work that we know can help our community.

As a black voice in a community I would say to parents that we should get together more. You might feel embarrassed if your neighbour knows that your child has been picked up by the police or go doing the wrong thing so you don't share it. People rather do keep it quiet. We should share more. It is quite possible to get some sort of consolation, some sort of comfort, some sort of advice if only you would communicate the problem to the right person. A leader, pastor, an older person with experience from the Caribbean, someone who knows the worth of prayer, who has had children of their own.

10

EDUCATION OR ALIENATION?

I could say many things about racism in schools. My own children suffered from time to time through being called insulting names. If they retaliated they were the ones to be reprimanded by the teachers. They complained often of teacher's racist remarks in school. The whole question of school and education has been hotly debated. People wonder if these things still happen but I can assure you that they do. The people who experience racism are made to feel they are stirring up trouble if they make an issue out of it most times. As if they go around looking for trouble.

My children have put up with a lot of insults. In one particular incident there were about seventy-five per cent ethnic minority children in the class and a teacher came in the class and said, 'Oh it's dark in here.' My daughter was sensitive and she picked it up. It ended up with an argument and the teacher took her to the head of the school. When she came home to me I did not give her the right for picking it up but I went to the head teacher, and tried to sort the trouble out. Explanations were given but the result was not satisfactory. I had to encourage my daughter and point out she needed a career, and sometimes must turn a deaf ear. She was a bright child.

Very bright. She knew the lesson but she never got asked. When it came to choosing options she had put down sport, needlework and office skills. I questioned why no examination subjects. What about higher education? I was told that she was not that bright. She was only fair. I took her away from that school and fought to get her in another one in the 'white highland' end of the borough. She now has a fair number of O-levels, three A-levels and studied at degree level.

We have to be strong and determined. We have to fight against racism for the black child to make a good grade at school. I had a lot of struggle steering my children through their education. They could have lost interest because of racist attitudes. I was careful enough to be always trailing across to school, giving them a lot of support, standing up for them. When they came home discouraged and crying I made sure I mended and healed them. I pointed out that under any circumstance they must learn. I was trying to say to them, 'I know this is happening but you've got to make it through it all. One of these days you won't be a student. You won't be a pupil. You will be an adult. You may even be a teacher.' They are educated now and can appreciate that was the best way to handle it.

I would call upon a lot more black parents to stand up for their children in school because if they don't the children are just left at the school gate to struggle on their own. There are teachers in school telling black children, 'You won't pass any exams. I don't know what your parents are worried about.' The impression was given that to sit exams was not necessary. Unfortunately that message has got home to one of my children and it's still affecting him today. I would say that the schools here have failed our children. It's only those who have real courage and a family that will push and stand up for them who will pull through the system successfully.

When my child was put down so that she wouldn't even have further education I determined that was not true and set out to prove to teachers that it wasn't. Black children would go through the entire school system in this country and at the end of the day pass through with no type of qualification at all. I'm not saying that it doesn't happen to some white children, but it is a fact that black children are not gaining the successes they ought. And of course this comes out when they seek employment. Give them a standard of education that will enable them to achieve good marks, go to university and be barristers, doctors, head teachers and other worthwhile professionals.

I have to give credit to the Swann report for what it has brought out about education among ethnic minorities. Being a leader in the community I know many of our young people did not achieve educationally, but not because they can't learn. When I was a child in the Caribbean, England set the exams and marked the papers and the children in the Caribbean were gaining passes. But if the same children arrived in England and continued their education here they would not be very successful. This is something that is of great concern.

A West Indian child arriving in this country and entering the classroom finds quite a difference. Not that the English language has changed, but you have to struggle with words pronounced in a different way. Children were having difficulties in really understanding what the teacher said so they had to learn at a slower pace. Because they were learning more slowly it was thought they weren't learning at all. This was swept under the carpet without anybody really looking at it and the long-term effect is coming out now. Some colleges and schools are realising the damage that was done but there is still a lack of awareness on the part of many schools. Most black children are losing confidence in white teachers.

My encouragement to staff is to change some attitudes and to involve black parents by giving them direct tasks to do. Change of attitudes can break down a lot of misunderstanding and barriers within communities and authorities. I have been going into schools long enough trying to increase awareness about the needs of black children. I've given talks to teachers at different times and had groups of children and teachers visiting the church and the club. I've talked to schools about how to get the black parents involved when they complain that black parents are not coming forth to be on the PTA or participate in the life of the schools.

We have to implement a lot of strategies to get people educated. When there is something wrong I speak to black parents. I say, 'We must sign a petition. We must go to the head of school.' I tell black people, 'You must get on the governing body. See what's going on with your children. Don't just leave them at the school gate. Give your children support.'

If the education system would allow more powerful leaders in the black community into the schools, to give an input, I'm sure a lot of black children would be helped and encouraged and would be coming out with more qualifications. The same children are coming out of the church to go to the schools. It's not just the teachers that are guiding and educating the child. The

Sunday School is doing it as well. I think there should be some sort of relationship between the churches and the schools.

I notice that a one-parent child at school would be referred to a psychiatrist quicker than any other child. I know that there are some marvellous one-parent families. Issues like that should be referred to one of the leaders in the community before calling in the psychiatrist. Mothers will come to us and ask us to see their children and have private talks and counselling with them. It helps. They are given understanding and the impression that somebody cares and will stand up with them. It's not just Mum. They are not alone.

Another thing that was not looked at was that in many classes there was a majority of white children and the two or three black children became isolated. They didn't just have to struggle with the isolation but with the whole situation of racism. When my children cried because they were called black at school I said, 'You should be proud. Just say to people, "Don't be jealous." ' I want them to be proud of who they are. This is the sort of foundation we should be laying down in our black children's consciousness because the community/society in which we live is not good at letting people be proud of who they are.

The right kind of history is not being taught. The education that is given in this country encourages white people to think they are better than black people. The books. *Robinson Crusoe. Master Willy has a roll in the mud.* The images. A black pig washing in the mud. I remember as a child some of the things I used to get in Sunday School. I wouldn't dare teach it now to a child. Blue-eyed, blonde Jesus, with white children round his knee and a black child with no clothes on sitting on the ground at his feet. It all reinforced the idea that white people were the masters. That had a damaging effect on me as a child yet I didn't see it until I came into this British society. Children who are born here are becoming sensitive to it. A lot of updating education needs to go on. They should get some black educationalists to handle the black issues in schools for the children not to be ashamed. The whole issue is about respect. Black children do not see many head teachers or many senior educationalists who are black. There are a few but it's not enough. Black children need a role model to be proud of, that they can follow.

Perched on the walls in schools all the pictures of up-front, forthcoming people are white. Or you get depressing photos of children starving in Africa and the Third World countries. I spent years in this country without seeing a black face on television from a positive viewpoint. My daughter is horrified when she sits in sociology lessons and listens to the negative things teachers are putting out about black countries and people. I believe there ought to be a campaign for better education within our schools and institutions about black people. Some of our children don't even know that black people were inventors, or take part in helping the economy of this country and the world. I taught my children what I knew but the schools should provide this. The books should be in museums and libraries.

I've been to one of my children's schools where all the black children were taken out of the class to go and learn culture. When I entered that classroom it was full of depressing photographs of Ethiopia and that sort of thing. Another child brought home to me a whole book on dialect, broken English, patwa, we call it back in the West Indies. That is in the villages back home. Not in areas where strong educational systems are established. I oppose these type of things. Experimenting has gone on with black children, even with those who are born here.

The schools in Britain should be really enhancing a programme for all the children in the school to let black children learn from their roots, their origins in a positive way. Cultures in a community are to enrich the whole community. If we're not going to accept each other's culture we can't live together. You hear governors of schools saying, 'Why do you want to teach in other people's language?' I wish I could have known other people's language when I travelled abroad. Every time you touch on strings like those the music blares. One of the things we should really be working on is to fight against this sort of racism in a whole educational setting. Though people are grown it doesn't mean that they are educated. Other cultures are important. It is important to an English person to hold on to their culture and it is more important to black people, living in a white society, to hold on to some of their culture. Culture has to do with education, with food, and with attitudes.

It's not a very easy process to accept each other's way of life. When I came into Britain it was difficult for me to stand in a queue in the shops or at the bus stop but I had to accept these things. I had to get used to the habit of drinking tea often and clocking in when I went to work. I had to eat British food, especially in the early days when there was no cultural food around. By doing this I have now come to enjoy the food. We have got to accept another culture once we live in it. At the same time I have no intention of giving up certain aspects of my culture, especially the food, though I have been living in Britain thirty years. Different cultures are something that adults should learn about and come to grips with. Unless that happens people won't respect each other.

I'm afraid we are going to come into a coconut age. Black outside and white inside. You break the coconut and you get down to whiteness. If people are steered properly there's no need for that. My children could have the same tendency. Not to want to eat my food. They're not in a white home but they're in a white culture, and it's the way people are taught. That's why I think schools should take on board respecting cultures from other countries. It's just a matter of accepting people and sharing their humanity. Let children recognise and identify their own background.

My children were born here but every so often we all go off to the West Indies together to let them see my roots, know where they belong, eat the food. They see their grandparents and their cousins and the way of life they live. From the time when they were small children I've taken them on trips back home to get that down in them. One of my girls went to Jamaica when she was about six or seven years of age. She came back with an exercise book with all her cousins' names and their ages. She had an eighty, ninety-year-old down to a child. And all the names of the food she ate. It was remarkable to see what she brought back for her scrapbook. The questions she asked. The information she found out. I once took over thirty young people back to the Caribbean with me to come face to face with their own roots. The youngsters lived in the context of a home, not as tourists, and I set up educational/social programmes across the island. The sense of freedom that they experienced and expressed was wonderful. When they wrote up the report it was grand. I think more young black children should be given a chance to see their roots. Not enough of that sort of education is done. A lot of the youngsters who were born here have not had the privilege of going to one of the countries back home.

My culture is dear to me and I try to let my children accept it. I live within my own culture in a lot of ways even in a white country so that my children can see and know about their roots. I am not so comfortable when a white person goes to a black country to study the culture then comes back to teach my children about it. I am able and capable of living the culture within the home for them to accept. If we don't then we will be looked on as if we are ashamed of our culture. I am not ashamed of the things that I grew up with in my own country and whenever I go back to the West Indies for a visit the culture is very, very dear to me. I still remember and love it.

When my daughter Sheila was about fourteen we were having a conversation and I was talking about the good old times back home at school. She then told us a story about 'back home' too. I said to her, 'Jamaica is not back home for you. Britain is your home.' She just turned and looked at me and said, 'No Mum. Home is where you are wanted.'

I didn't teach her this. I didn't impose it on her. I have always had white people as friends coming in and fellowshipping and spending days in my home. I believe it's because she's been back to Jamaica. She saw the culture. The food. The way of life. And she saw it being lived out in the home there. It's an identity. Home is where you are comfortable. When I come home I throw off my shoes and put on my slippers and sit with my feet up. Stretch out on the settee. Switch on the television. Open the fridge. If I came to visit you I wouldn't do that. I would be in your house. That's how she feels. She knows what she is talking about. She goes to school and she sees it in the school and the clubs. Society forces this on them. It has rejected them and because of this they don't feel a sense of belonging and many of them will fight back.

11

A HIDDEN AGENDA

It is not the same walking around in Britain under a black skin. I have been told that I don't belong here and should go back so many times I have lost count. I want to feel part of society/community, but I can't help being aware that rejection is there each time I walk down the road. Many people won't accept that Britain is multi-cultural. I've been to school, to evening classes, to Bible College. Some folks wouldn't sit beside me. They wouldn't talk to me. Some of us never knew there was such a thing as racism until we entered Britain. There were class barriers but that's not so damaging. Even though white people lived in our land and made their homes there they were still very separate. The black people would work for them but there was no mixture there. Even the ministers had to be 'missus' and 'master.' They wouldn't mix as equals. They had their own clubs and venues for entertainment. Black girls and boys would be working for white people but they wouldn't drive them in their car, even to take them to the market to buy food. I opposed that kind of behaviour from a young age.

Despite this we could still get jobs. We could be working alongside a white person getting the same money.

People like ourselves who come from Jamaica were living in mixed communities. We were living next to white people. This is why the culture shock was so terrible for me. I was just thrown in the deep end in this country. All of a sudden. We began to see colour when we were called black. When we were put down. We saw the slogans on the wall. People got up from beside us on the bus. I knew there was a hostility in people towards me. Conflict. It was strange to discover it was because of colour. We were called names and insulted, not just by strangers, but by people we worked beside. They would make remarks like, 'Black people ought to go home' and 'This place is swamped with blacks'.

These were some of the shattering things for black people. For me especially. To think how naive we were. When I came to London and saw white people shopping and scrubbing the floor and cleaning the street I couldn't believe my eyes. I thought everyone would have servants, like back home. It just told me it was because Jamaica was a black country they behaved in that manner. It stimulated some of us to conclude that these things were coming out of racism, the whole colonialism episode. All this 'Come to Britain,' was only to exploit black people.

Later on we heard remarks from the Prime Minister and people like Enoch Powell. Then we had the Immigration and Nationality Bill to contend with. It was an insult to us. I remember when folks began to come to England when I was a child they never had to go for visas. They just booked their fare and travelled. Even when I came I didn't have to have a certificate of entry or anything. I had a passport. It says BRITISH right across it.

Not long after I came we listened to the announcements that we had to officially register. It didn't cost a lot in those days but it was a gradual process until now it is possible to lose the right of registration. It might have been a long time before the final date but some people were still not aware. A lot of folks from the Third World who are living here did not come out to be registered as British citizens. People are fearful of the things they don't know. To me there's a hidden agenda behind it all which has never been made plain. It has affected black countries most so one cannot say it's not a black and white issue. Injustice in the laws really disappointed many of us. We were always told the history of our mother country at school. I had this concept of coming home. When these immigration and nationality laws began to slam down I began to feel it was a mother who didn't want her children.

Eggs have been thrown at me and bags of flour have been thrown from vehicles. My face has been slapped. These events are not just from years ago. It is happening today. Now. In the community where I've lived and worked for over fourteen years. Just months ago my car was painted all over with 'NF' and all sorts of slogans. The very street we live on is not a safe place to walk. One black lady had just left church in the middle of the daytime, three o'clock, well dressed, when a car drove up on the pavement and someone slashed her across the back with something very sharp. Two more elderly ladies were leaving church not long ago and were hit by some very hard articles, possibly golf balls. We don't feel safe. Yet every time we say these things people say it happens to white people as well. It's not the same.

I have experienced black and white Christians meeting for worship events and conferences to talk about racial harmony but when those same people meet you on the street they pretend they've never seen you before. One Sunday I was preaching on suffering in a church. I mentioned my own experience of rejection, insults, discrimination. A woman in the congregation stormed, 'You people look for these things.' The minister had to assure the congregation it happens and give examples he knew. Incidents like this have not changed for the better. When somebody denies the experience we have as black people dealing with racism that's unfair. I spent a number of years trying to bring the community together before I came out in the limelight. I've been fighting racism at school with teachers and the children for a long time. I know stories of Asian children taking their lunch to school and the dinner lady making havoc by criticising what they had, instead of putting it on a plate and giving it to them. They had to hide it under the table to eat.

Some of us managed to struggle through the system and help our children but it was not easy. There has been the constant going up to school each time they came home with a complaint, changing children from one school to another. When black people tried to get their children in some schools they were refused. Even the church schools are guilty of this. Some of our children have dropped out of education completely because of harassment. The education that is given in this country sets up white people to be better than black people. The type of books, the photographs that are used. The kind of books that should be bought for black children to grow up and read should be to influence and determine their future. The whole question of racism is damaging in all aspects in this country. Those of us who lived through the pain of rejection and prejudice would not want this to happen to the children who are born here. We want them to be able to feel at home. I believe it's because of ignorance that people don't realise it's wrong to treat a person who is a different colour with less dignity or respect. This society will have to drastically change some of the attitudes shown to black people otherwise the children who are born here will feel uncomfortable and angry. Some of us who came here thirty years ago like myself have coped with the racism, the bad housing, the low-paid jobs. We worked and we achieved and many have gone back to their countries.

But what about those black people who are born here, whose roots are in Britain? How are we going to steer them to cope with the racism that is in this country? They are born into the system. They go to school. They are marrying, having children. They are working now. They pay taxes. They are standing up in various areas of community life, serving on committees, making plans. They are training themselves to be a part of this society. They are not going to take it so easy. It's going to cause problems.

When I was homeless once I was given a house where the toilet was outside. There was only one wash-basin. A little one in the kitchen. I had young children and my husband worked nights sometimes. When I pointed this out to the housing department they thought I was well off to get that. So I told myself I had to provide for myself and my family. But I don't think my child who is born here is going to take things like that very easy. I am afraid there will be blood shed in Britain if those people who are British by birth are not accepted. All that makes me British is a registration number but my children were born here. It's where they belong. They are not going to take the things that we took lying down.

There are different conflicts and hostilities within communities and people of different cultures but the black and white issue stands out more than any of the others. This is why I want to fight against racism. It stares you in the face. As long as I live in Britain I will have to champion the cause of right and wrong, of peace and justice. Every person has a right to feel that they are human and a right to live as equals. While I am in this country it's a fight that is on my hands. I started off because of the attitude of people towards me. Now I am looking ahead on the younger generation that are born here.

For some people coming to Britain has proved to be a wrong decision. It's been damaging. Especially for those who came from humble villages and now have to live in the inner cities. It has not done them or their children the best. Some have made it. If you are prepared to compromise. If you are prepared not to be involved in justice and peace, race relations, racism. To shut that out of your mind. I can't. I have very interesting and good white friends but at the same time regrettably racism still exists around me. It doesn't matter what job I hold. It doesn't matter where I live. I cannot shut it out. Neither could my children. It's going to be a continuing battle and some of us will have to fight.

There are more complicated issues to do with race than just those small insulting behaviours. When something is wrong within the black community the way it is put across by some of the papers does not help to create a good image. The media paint it worse. It's taken on board and related to the public as if such a thing has never happened before. I'm sure all these prisons in Britain were built long before black people came to this country. In every race you find criminals, murderers, rapists, whatever. I feel hurt when people say, 'But you're not like the others, are you?' That's patronising. I am like the others. Humanity is not different.

The media don't do well for black people. At all. We're not told the good stories. It makes us feel as if we want to go back. Those of us who have to live together, black and white, in the inner city situations, like in London, know that what the media are saying is not true. We know it is damaging to good practices, to relationships. We are the cutting edge. We have seen it. But what about people who live in the white highlands? Who have not come across any black people? Who don't know our style of life and behaviour? Who only know black people by what the media portray? Tottenham is burning down. Black people are burning Toxteth, or Brixton.

When I talked to the indigenous community about the riots they behaved as if riots had never been known in this country before. If people read their history they would know there were riots long before black people lived here. Black people are being stereotyped and marginalised. They are not seen as individuals. All are put into one boat. Unless you are a Jesse Jackson or Desmond Tutu who stands out. I suppose they too go down the road mugging? There are upfront brilliant people. Tutu. Martin Luther King. Courageous. Fighting for the cause of humanity. And yet you don't see their photographs flashing all over the place as heroes.

Or hear of the achievements that take place in the lives of black people.

Most times you don't get these things portrayed in British society. You're more likely to read an article in the papers about West Indians not having books in their homes. It's so wrong. The journalist has probably only gone to one or two West Indian families. I'm sure they've got the books in their homes but not in the living room. The cultures are different. I've got hundreds of books packed all over my place. Books in my library. Books in the bedroom. Books in my kitchen. The only place you wouldn't find books is in my living room. I don't want my living room to look like a library. My favourite books are packed around me in my bedroom for reading at night. My children's bedrooms have a bookshelf. They're not just there to display, to tell people that we read. I have over four thousand books but I don't have them piled in my living room. I don't even want to put a television in my living room for that matter. It's a place that I can go and put my feet up and be quiet. To say West Indians don't have books is ridiculously stupid. This is the kind of image people would quickly write about black people. They stereotype. People's perceptions of black people are just out of ignorance.

12

INCIDENTS AND INSTITUTIONS

The images that are painted in this country of black people are very unwise and very unfair. If you have a headline about immigrants, when you start to read down the lines it ends up with black people and poverty and depression. The Church gets it wrong too. Sad to say. I've been looking on some posters from some Christian organisations portraying black people as beggars who have nothing. In the past Britain has taken everything they have from some of these countries that are begging today. They're not actually begging Britain. They're saying, 'Bring back some of what you have taken.'

Some people only see us as beggars and poverty-stricken people. That's the image. We get fed up of seeing about the needs of the ethnic minority in reports and committees, newspaper and television. Everybody has a need. There are poor white people in this country. All we are saying is treat everybody with fairness. Fair in jobs and housing. Fair in education. Fair across the whole level of human life.

To hear people saying, 'We don't have a problem because there are no black people living out here,' kills you. Straightaway. It damages. They are saying the problem is with the black people rather than the systems and the policies that swallowed up some of us in this country. Most people like myself have worked hard and provided for our children. We do not want to see houses burning, riots in the street. These things are coming out of frustration and the need to fight back. People are not looking at the frustrations. The unemployment in the inner city. The prejudice. The substandard housing conditions. The ghetto that the housing people cause in their own towns and cities. Black and ethnic organisations that try to develop community projects have to creep and beg and fawn on local government and other agencies to give some money to help. It's a long-drawn-out harassment. The systems of this country are only ready to act when the horse has gone through the gate. Authorities should not wait for communities to get overturned with riots, anger and desperation before they begin to treat everybody on fair grounds.

My daughter has worked in a big store in London ever since she left school. She knows the job. She's been trained to do it. She has reached the place where she trains other people. They promote those she has trained and leave her. It happened to me also. I sat for two and a half weeks teaching somebody to do the job I was doing. Once that white person got hold of the job they demoted me. Local authorities take a white middle class person and give them a big post in an inner city situation making decisions to deal with the needs of ethnic minorities without the presence of the ethnic minorities themselves. It doesn't make sense. There are people who have the same qualifications but their colour prevents them getting the job.

The process for a plural, just and fair society takes longer because people become evasive instead of getting right to the solution. Those who have never travelled, never lived with black people, who have no real experience of what kind of people we are, just look at us and estimate us by the colour of our skin. That hurts. Because we are black we stand less chance of getting the type of jobs that should help us to develop our families, to buy the right house, to progress like any other person. When we move into an area we know our property will be devalued because black people are living there.

These are real situations. That is why we have to stand up in the struggle and fight to change people. I once thought it was just behaviour patterns which led to our being called names on the street and dubbed the lowest of the low by people in the community where we worked and lived. Then when I began to study at college I was able to look at how systems and institutions work in this country. It all came together. I realised it's not just the names I'm called that affects me. It digs deeper than that. It's the institutional, organised racism that is a danger to black people in this country; when we are deprived of the right jobs, the right housing, the right education.

Look at equal opportunities. Who sits on the interviewing panels? Who holds the top jobs in housing, education, social services? Who holds the office of bank manager? Head of school? Who are the bosses? Who are on the decision-making committees in institutions, churches, whatever? Look at all these things and you will see who holds the power. The policies of the system have to change and they have to change at the top. The battle is between the rich and the poor, the powerful and the powerless.

There are educated and successful black people who

are still not able to get the right jobs. This raises many questions. Interviews are still conducted by mainly white, male, middle-class panels rather than a cross-section of the community. The experience black teachers have from white staff and the way they are promoted are issues that need looking at. They have just elected one of the first black chief inspectors in schools. She shared with us that when she was introduced in the canteen as inspector somebody said, 'London Transport is doing fine.'

This is happening today. Although black people are moving up the scale our white counterparts are still not accepting and respecting the reality of equality. Sometimes we go two steps from down below and things begin to change in some areas. There are good stories to tell. Relationships begin to develop. It seems we are getting somewhere peaceably, only to see some horrible story in the paper or on television in the morning. A person with influence in society just has to say one thing against the black community and that's it. Folk don't think for themselves and have their own opinion. They jump on the bandwagon and follow the crowd. These are things that weary one. Some leaders are trying their best to bring about a peaceful society but others set out to spoil every good practice. The fight is on and it's long. There is a lot of training and educating to do. It's slow and people are waiting for the wrong opportunity before they get going. Racism must be tackled by black and white. Parents, authorities, schools, colleges, politicians, and churches should be in this battle now. All together. Working jointly to shape our communities.

If the white people think black people are going to disappear from this land it's a myth. They are not going to disappear. Many more black people are going to be born in this country. The numbers are going to grow. One day we will find black people in positions like Jesse Jackson running for Prime Minister. America has more years than us in the fight for freedom and equality, but the fight has begun in this country. And it will continue. There are going to be stronger people than myself when I'm off the scene. It's going to be a constant campaign. One cannot deny the fact that the black people who are born here are belonging and need to feel a sense of belonging.

I know America has a long history and a long fight but I believe one day they are going to get there. The assassination of Martin Luther King was something which made me feel that I should fight this cause more, and that some of us might have to die to stand up for the right. Martin Luther King is one of the pioneers I admire a lot. In his last speech he said about when black children and white children would walk hand in hand. You couldn't want a greater mission than that. If Christians in this country, white and black, come together in unity with one voice, seeking out a way to achieve justice and peace, not only in words but in action, then the dream will come true. Hand in hand, black and white will walk together. But the wheel takes so long to turn when it comes to race issues. It's not done genuinely because people see there is a need and it's going to help to change evil practices. We have to fight and put pressure on.

A lot of people have heard the word racism but it's in a bracket. The people who are real racists do not even understand that racism is when one nation believes they are better than the other and believing that they show it in their attitudes. There is a need to help people understand they cannot really fight racism as a white person unless they discover their own racism. What should be done at this stage is to educate people about racism and how much it hurts. In the early eighties things began to happen. More pressure groups developed. Race relations groups were set up dealing with community and culture and taking on the whole problem of racism. But we are still coming up against some very difficult times when we tackle racism as a subject in workshops or seminars. There are some people who are deliberately not prepared to understand. They would put down their attitude to something else. They are embarrassed in dealing with racist issues. If we bring out our own personal experience of how racism affects us that's not accepted. If we bring it out in history, colonialism and the whole issue of exploitation, that also is rejected.

One of the things I will not accept is when white people say, 'When you talk about racism it's counter-productive.' Racism is evil. It's like a cancer that eats at people and destroys them. If you don't do something it stays there and gets into every generation that is coming up. We have made a late start but it must be tackled. It's causing a lot of problems for people who want to get on in communities and live their lives with respect and dignity.

You've got to work on your own doorstep. Grass roots level is one of the best places to start because you have to live there. You have to deal with the people. Your neighbourhood, your community is of vital importance. You've got to face your neighbour and those in the community every day. You have to go to the shop. You have to go to the petrol station. You have to go to the post office. Local involvement matters so much and is where a great deal of the hurt and embarrassment is caused. It takes a lot of effort to pull things together at grass roots level.

At the same time whatever happens up top has an effect because that's where the streams run from. I believe that it's about time British politicians, influential people in government and church leaders were doing more to improve what grass roots people are working on. This is where the church has an influence and should use it. A white person can help another white person to be aware of their racism more than I, being a black person, can.

It's out of ignorance that white people in this country talk about feeling threatened or that black people are taking over. Comparing the numbers of black people to white people there are just a fraction. The powerful jobs, the seat of power, chambers of power are dominantly white. White people are the masters of the schools. They are the head of the police, head of the armed forces. They are the politicians. How can white people say they feel threatened? Just the presence of black people in a community can't threaten white people. What is needed to come closer to a plural society is for people to accept each other as human beings and share their humanity with each other. People need to realise that though we are not of the same colour we have the same emotions, the same joys and tears. We are made equally by God. Race issues should be tackled from a Christian viewpoint, especially in a country that claims to be Christian.

13

THE GROWTH OF THE BLACK-LED CHURCHES

I want to fight this race issue but not without God. That's where I find my strength and courage. That's where you get the humility. That's where you get the real antidote for the sort of tragedies we have to face. I want to thank God for Christian faith and with it the power of forgiveness. Hate is a burden. Especially for me. I never carry a grudge. Though when I discovered that Jesus said we are to love our enemies the first thing that came to me was, 'You must be joking. How can I love those who hurt me?' It was one of the most frightening things when I read the scripture and realised what it was saying to me. I couldn't grasp it in my ignorance when I was going through the pain and the struggle. I could have hated people and of course I wanted to hate. I could have been a person who was unable to get over some of the hurt that has been inflicted had it not been for the love, the peace, the forgiveness that comes with the faith. The word of God changed me. On the inside. The only time the Bible is effective is when it becomes alive, out of your experience, when you try to live it.

We are hurt because we are human. It hurts, even to tell some of the stories. It's something that needs a lot of meditation and prayer. It is a constant battle but I can live in this country now and feel some measure of freedom with those I work and live and have to deal with in my everyday life. I will protest. I will campaign. I will help people to be aware of their own racism. Rather than to hate or fight back with violence or any kind of physical battles.

Young people are not so tolerant. They cannot understand why they should go through all the hurts and aches and pains inflicted on them because they are born black. They are saying, 'Why was I born like this? Why should this happen?' We have to find answers to give them. They know they are not responsible for the colour of their skin. We have got to be working on that area with our children to help them understand and accept their blackness. And be proud and use it positively. I did that in my own family when Jackie was very hurt when she was called black at school. It took time for it to get home to her but the other children laid off when she began to shout, 'Yes, I'm black, and why are you jealous?'

It's very powerful for those that the sermon is coming home to, as it is in the black-led churches. The black Pentecostal Church has provided for the young, for middle-aged, for old, a sense of identity, equality, participation. Young people don't need to go out and plait their hair in dreadlocks to find identity. They identify themselves with whatever is going on. They are part of it. So however criticised the black-led churches are they have this value and the story must be told. A tremendous amount of young people were born and brought up within the Church. We were not able to hold a majority of them but quite a number are still with the Church. Some are ordained to ministries. Many are held by the gospel music, which is catching. It is something for them to look forward to, and it brings out their skills and keeps them together.

For a long time other churches tended not to see the function of the black-led churches in this country but while they were ignoring these new groups we were growing. What was happening in East London developed in other boroughs. The growth continued to be tremendous in the fifties, sixties and seventies until today we find a fast growing movement. It is one of the most powerful and dynamic organisations of black people in this country and has been one of the fastest growing churches in Britain for the past ten years.

One could say the black-led churches are not united but the white-led churches are the same. In the early days when there were only eight or ten black-led churches in London we were more unified, meeting together every week. But now there are many, in the thousands, all over the country and it's difficult to know, or support, every one. They function on a different ident-ity of names. The Church of God in Christ, the Church of God of Prophecy, the Church of the First Born, the Apostolic churches, the New Testament Assembly to which I belong and hundreds more. The New Testament Church of God is one of the largest. The New Testament Assembly originated in the West Indies and then spread to Britain, Africa, America and Canada, as did most of the others.

It should not be expected that all the black-led churches in this country could ever function under one umbrella. We have differences of doctrine and belief but the whole teaching and experience of Christians from the black-led churches is based upon the Bible and we understand each other and worship and fellowship together. Though we function under different names we are together in spirit and over the past four years we have developed groupings. The Afro-West Indian United Council of churches, the West Indian Evangelical Alliance, the black pastors' conference and the national black clergy consultative group. These four groupings can pull together almost all the black-led churches in England. It suddenly dawned upon the other churches that we were an Army as well, though they had never recognised us through three decades in this country. I think awareness has grown rapidly over the past five years with the issues we raised with the British Council of Churches, to do with resources and the purchasing of buildings for instance. It is still very difficult for the black-led churches to own buildings because of the competition from commercial buyers and the way the whole thing is handled. When we are allowed to use church buildings we struggle with the high rents charged and the many rules and regulations imposed. For two of our buildings at the moment we are paying over £2000 a month for a mortgage. We have finished paying for the building in which I am now worshipping but it has become too small to house the congregation. When I moved to Leyton there were about thirty of us. Today we have over two hundred people. We started to negotiate for larger premises but the asking price just went up and up out of our reach. We had to take a smaller building because of insufficient funds. Even buildings that are breaking down are not offered at a reasonable price to the black churches. I am not asking that they should be given to us for nothing but at least some sympathy should be shown towards other Christians.

As we raised these issues more and more people began to be aware that we were here and were not just a few. The handbook for the black-led churches was finished and put out and that helped too. People began to realise that the black-led churches had now spread in Britain and grown in numbers. I am sure that if the black-led churches had not sprung up in response to a time of need many more people would possibly have been in mental homes or hospitals or prisons because of the pressure they were passing through. Some people would not have a faith today. The black-led churches were like open arms for us. We had nobody to turn to for encouragement, for strength, for prayer and for Christian counselling except the Church. The ministry that runs within the black-led churches in this country should not be underestimated. I just feel grateful for the platform, the recognition, the identity, the quality of the work done by these churches. We are not separatist but it is difficult to get white people to settle under black leadership. We have a few. Not many. This is something I'm exploring. We have something to offer and it's for all people. I feel very proud of the work and the trend the black-led churches have taken. Valuable work is being done especially in the inner city among the lonely, the depressed, the deprived. the sick. When contacted in times of emergency the black-led churches are always ready to serve. The minister and lay people will go into homes and institutions to encourage people and help them. The black-led churches take their Christianity very seriously. We don't place emphasis on the word 'religion'. Our concerns are about being saved, born again, changed. Once you're changed you will want to tell others. People spread the story in the lift, on the stairs, on the buses and trains, in the shops, in the market place. Wherever people are. This is one of the reasons why the black-led churches are growing so fast. It's the face-to-face, down-to-earth, spontaneous way of relating Christianity to other people in ordinary places.

We have found that many people who came to Britain and were rejected by the white churches have since lost their faith and are wandering round somewhere in the community. Many of these people have been rescued by the black-led churches. The church provides fellowship, sharing, friendship and love which is needed so badly within communities. Our churches have served in the capital city in a remarkable way. Some of our people have not studied, or achieved great academical skills but yet they have managed to contribute an abundance of valuable service through various networks, including the churches. These people deserve a lot of credit.

We feel we must struggle on, even if we don't get money from the government or trusts or grant-making bodies. We've got to make it. We've got to go on. We're a self-help group of people that have no resources. Most times we survive by free will offerings and donations by our own people. The black-led church has achieved everything through self-help, whether acquiring buildings and colleges, or developing social projects. I met the Prime Minister some time ago. Possibly my name came in front of her through the various committees on which I have served. It was a lovely evening, a formal gathering, but down-to-earth, practical conversation took place. I raised some of the things that are happening in the inner city and how the cut-backs are affecting the underprivileged, and had her word of assurance that people will have to help themselves.

For years I think white Christians looked on the black-led churches as a bunch of noisy people. It may be so but within that noise the heart of God is there. At the heartbeat of the church. Today we are slightly less harassed. Some communities have accepted the preaching, the singing and the music. We believe in worshipping God by making a joyful noise just like the Bible says. When you come together to express yourself before the Lord you should be free to cry and laugh, to express your emotions. As long as it is done in order.

We are not asking people who do not like noise to change their quiet way of worship. I could put up with worshipping down the road in the parish church for an hour quietly but when it comes to the time when I feel I must shout I will have to find somewhere to shout. We should not have to adapt to the way of worship within the institutional churches in order to work alongside them. I do not have to become an Anglican to worship with Anglicans, or a Methodist to worship with Methodists. We have much to learn from each other in our different ways of expressing our love and worship to God. The black-led churches should be appreciated for putting the fire back into Britain's religion. I am glad to be one of those Christians who can shout Hallelujah to express my love for God without being subdued by traditions and programmes. I am sure that in the kingdom of God when all the millions of Christians shall end up finally in heaven there is going to be a great noise.

14

WOMEN IN THE CHURCH

The church is not a one-man band. It's everybody together. Women make a marvellous contribution leading the worship, administering, serving the church at every level with commitment and faithfulness. When there are celebrations the women work hard preparing the meals, baking, decorating, organising whatever you put them to do. They fill up the choir seats. They clean the church. They arrange the flowers, care for the communion sets, work in the Sunday school and youth department, guide young people in the right way of marriage, and support the church physically and financially. In all these activities in most congregations it is the women who are the majority. In some congregations the minister or a deacon is the only man. Many of the husbands are not coming forth and getting involved in church life. You'll find them in the pub. I will some day write a book entitled, 'Where are the men?'

Looking at women's ministry in the black-led churches and in my own denomination I can say that within the hierarchy there is no difference in the ministry of men and women. Women conduct the ordinances, and officiate at marriages and communion. I was surprised to read in the newspaper not long ago of the first woman to perform a marriage in this country until I realised it was talking about the Church of England. In my own denomination, the New Testament Assembly, there can be traces of prejudice against women officiating as pastors and leaders, differences of opinion about it, but it is not so open. It would be subtle and just among a few, the minority. Some black-led churches already have women bishops. Whether or not this will happen in my denomination is still to be seen. If it does happen I am sure it would not cause an explosion though it would raise questions and mark history for the New Testament Assembly. In my denomination baptism is done by immersion. The officiating of this act by women is challenged by the men. They sometimes argue it is not a woman's place to go in the water. I cannot accept that a woman should be exempt from such activities. Biblically there is neither male nor female when it comes to the kingdom of God. I have not seen anything indicating that a woman cannot perform certain ceremonies without a man.

Ministry however has always been looked upon as a male system, male dominated. Men's view of God seems to be a big man who sits there on the throne. Some preachers make it look as if he's saying no women, no women. Working alongside bishops and priests at ministerial level is a painful experience. It is very difficult being a woman and black within a white system. People can be so patronising. All too often when I sit on a committee I am the only woman, the only black face. This is one of the areas which needs looking at seriously. I am not fighting for myself, but I'm in the struggle with other women who would want to find themselves in equal participation in the ministry. Women have got to learn to overcome fears and doubts and be more open to speak on these issues. There is still a lack of awareness on the part of men. Most times if you are participating in a service the last thing that some men would ask you to do is to be the preacher. They might ask you to pray or to read the scripture but the preacher is invariably male. I'm wondering what is happening. It is an awful shame. Men and women study in the same college, take the same courses, achieve on equal levels but there is discrimination when it comes to ordination and participation.

Sympathetic men might brand me a pioneer to see women reach some sort of recognition in the church because I am always fighting for women's rights. But at the end of the day it is men who say that women should remain in their place. I have a question to ask. 'Where is the place of women? Where should a woman be, if it is not in the kingdom of God?' Many women feel as if they are trapped within the church and within society. They have to struggle because it is forced upon them.

I am not trapped. I am free inside and out. The freedom I am talking about is that inner freedom. I am married and this to me is not a prison. I have conversations with women who still feel they are second place and that they should not be doing the things men do. Some women still think they should give their husband the best and eat less than the man eats. All these concepts that are held by a lot of women are embedded in the West Indian community. The man is the breadwinner. The wife's place is in the house. My own mother never went out. My father was the one who went out to preach or visit friends or do the shopping.

Even today if the husband shares equally in the housework with his wife some people criticise him and say he is a funny man. His wife has done something to him. I am very much in sympathy with women across the world who have been made to feel that they are second class and slaves to men. I enjoy a marriage of sharing and I believe that is what God meant marriage to be. We share in every sense. Joys, happiness, everyday activities, burdens, workloads, sorrows. Usually it's the woman who takes on the extra stress and workload. I saw a lot of that in my parents' marriage when I was a child. In this day and age there is no such thing as the husband being 'My lord.' If I am out somewhere I don't have to make a special effort to rush home to prepare the meal. Times have changed and we must adapt to those changes.

If we are just going to fight against external structures it is a false way of obtaining freedom and liberation. Without this equal participation in marriage and the various forms of ministry there will always be disputes. There would be more happiness and comfort in marriage if the woman felt she was not just a slave but was working and living alongside the man on equal terms. Perhaps then many marriages, including Christian marriages, would have lasted rather than ending in divorce.

This is not just a lesson for society, it is a lesson for the Church. Sharing on equal terms is not yet practised. Too often we listen to words, or read a book telling us that women's place is in the kitchen. If that's the truth then I would ask every wife to teach her husband to cook. If the communion is only for men to administer why train women for ministry within the Church? Let us look away from the long past of traditions and embark upon a mission of sharing. The first step towards free-

113

dom is to get out of the system that has taken women over for so many years. We have seen it in our parents and grandparents. We have seen it in the Church. We have seen it in society. It has become part of our lives. If it can be overcome from the heart then we are on our way to freedom. In the Church I experience total freedom to work alongside men as their equal. I do not see myself as being in bondage or trapped. I feel quite free and confident. I do not feel in any way out of place carrying out the same ordinances as my male partners. I believe I am in my rightful place sharing in the mission of God's kingdom. Although I'm constantly challenged as a woman I do not feel threatened. I know I am being of service for the kingdom. I am called by the Lord. I have an inner assurance that God is with me and is blessing what I do. I do not share the view of some theologians that God would not call a woman or let that view impinge on my service and work. I am confident deep inside that God is pleased with the things I am doing, and I want to see other women who are torn between these conflicts having sufficient confidence in themselves to do the things they want for Christ.

I know it can happen that women find themselves in situations where they have to struggle. When people campaign against the ordination of women this surely must make women feel they are trapped. I would not belong to an organisation which kept a lid on me so that I had to fight to be what I am. I have blessings to give to women who are still fighting with the awful tragedy and evil of inequality, especially within the church. I want to say to them, be bold, carry on, oppose the crushing down of women as if to say they are low and men are high. I want to encourage women in this fight.

It is a battle that must be won. There is going to be a song of victory for the women. They will not be held down for ever. Women are going to have power. Women will be ordained and be equal servants in the ministry with men. Not just when we get to heaven but here on earth.

In some denominations they have deliberately separated ministries for women, calling it the women's ministry. Women can participate in leading the service during the weekdays but these services are attended only by women. This is happening universally. I have recently returned from Africa where I was speaking at a meeting conducted by women. Only women attended the meeting although it was an ordinary service of worship and praise. Not one man was present. I was invited to preach at that church and was told that had it not been for the women's night I might not have been able to participate.

Women's ministry is not something that should be separated from other ministries within the Church. When it comes to domestic and family life and the bringing up of children women are more than capable, but when it comes to ministry we are told we must forget all that. Whatever a man can do to build the kingdom of God, spread the gospel, offer worship and praise, preach and teach, I firmly believe that a woman can also fulfil effectively. I would not be content to belong to a separate 'women's ministry' in the Church. I hope that women will look again at that little corner of the Church where they have been pushed and be careful that they are not really accepting a defeat when it comes to working and standing up for the kingdom of God.

Women have got to be strong, to be bold, to be fearless to really gain freedom from those historical images of men being the lord over women. We can so easily be crushed by attitudes. In some jobs if we hold a position higher than men they do not respect us and we can tell that by the way they speak. In most cases it is because the men feel threatened. I want to say to women who have risen to power or leadership, 'Just live out your life as a person. You can be strong yet charming. You can hold power with wisdom. This is what makes you the woman who will champion a good cause. You do not need to use your strength and ability to crush your partner or your colleagues. Women must not be afraid.'

15

PASTORAL MINISTRY

Men can accept women in certain roles in the Church but some refuse to accept them as pastors. When I am addressed as pastor by certain folk this comes as a real surprise. A few black women are pastoring their own churches in Britain but in most cases these are congregations pioneered by the women themselves. Some of the large black-led churches are not ordaining women as pastors even if they are working at leadership level. They are called ministers, not pastors.

Women should not be separated from pastoral ministry. I have been serving in the pastoral ministry for over fifteen years and know of other women who are also ordained as pastors and their ministry is successful. Women are well able to undergo the stresses and strains and can understand particularly intricate difficulties concerning the family like bereavement, overcrowding, homelessness, the woman whose child is missing without trace, loneliness, economical stress, marriage break-up. We meet these problems daily in our jobs as social worker, welfare officer, woman police constable, teacher. Why not as pastor?

All the stresses put together mean some folk can hardly draw themselves along to sit down on a Sunday.

They are drained. A person sometimes carries pressures, burdens and stress for a whole week. I have tried many times to write my sermons and to go in the pulpit and preach from notes but it doesn't work. People don't want to come and sit down and hear about the football team or a lecture in theology. They need to hear that they have a friend who loves them, who cares for them. That means something. They need to see it in practice after the service is finished; to feel an arm round their shoulder, a welcome, a song in the spirit that touches their emotions, and allows them to cry.

There's a ministry I depend upon within the Pentecostal Church. That is where people get together and although they're praying and crying, some of them as loud as they can, you hear your name going up in prayer before God. People take you to heart so much you just feel they are sharing your problems and you are able to come out victorious. I know it is emotional and many white people don't like to be emotional, but don't take away the hallelujahs and 'praise the Lord' and dancing and clapping. I shall never forget how a white lady came to our church once and because she saw us holding each other, putting our arms around each other, having a little kiss, she thought all the ladies were lesbians or involved in something immoral. It was so strange to her.

I feel when you get to the pulpit you are not preaching to prove how eloquently you can speak. I was still studying when I was forty and many of the black pastors in this country have a good theological background. I'm not saying there is anything wrong with that. If so I was mad to sit in college for so many years. Nevertheless I am in the pulpit to reach people. So that people can feel that they are getting something to feed their spiritual soul, their life. When they leave church they need a memory for when they are sunken down in depression. A simple song. A message. Sometimes in the service I just say, 'Would you like to take somebody by the arm? Turn around and say, "I love you." ' Some people just live with an animal at home. A cat or a dog. They haven't contact with anybody. Others go to work and come in too tired to do anything but go to bed. Coming out on Sunday they have the chance to meet others, to chat and share. People want to talk out their frustrations.

Sometimes I can actually stand in the pulpit and read the needs of the congregation. I remember one time when I was worshipping abroad everybody looked so miserable and far apart from each other. I had just come in for a few minutes to say 'Hello Jesus' and go back through the door so I asked the congregation to turn around and get acquainted with each other, to look someone in the face and see if they could manage a smile. There was so much emotion, so many tears. I didn't have to preach. Sometimes people are next to tears but they put on a brave face. As a pastor I can go up and just gently put my hand on folks and the next thing is a bundle of tears. It's nice when you have a shoulder to cry on and feel safe. Emptying it makes such a difference. You can do this in the context of Christian caring and loving one another. It's one of the ways some people manage to survive.

If you don't reach people through your sermon you must reach them socially or by some other means. I believe Jesus used a lot of styles and some of the things he did if he was here today people would complain about. One of the facts about Jesus is that he knew just where the needs were. I feel if I want to pattern anybody, if I want a model of what ministry really should be, it would be Jesus. I must confess that many times I forget what was taught me in college.

We have developed now in most of the Pentecostal churches not just to have a long message and singing and send people home. We have a meal. It's not just my family, my husband and children sharing a meal. It might be a disabled person who can't go home and manage to cook by themselves, somebody who hasn't got heating, a single person who lives on their own, someone who is not working, with very little money to buy a proper meal. They can share and not feel like a stranger. Eating together is a whole sort of tradition which is very much needed. Especially in the inner cities.

As a pastor I get to know a lot more than other people would know. I have an opportunity of getting closer to the problems. People will share their sorrows, share their frustrations and financial needs. I can't just stand there and not do something about them. When I see families breaking apart and I know children are going to suffer I tend to want to do something. Problems are always tumultuous. I see a young couple with three children living in one room and it's spoiling the relationship between the man and his wife. I know they're not in a position to buy a house of their own and they're not likely to receive council housing. I meet large families with very little money. Children are underfed. The young wife can't afford to buy a new dress or pair of shoes. Father tries but cannot get a job. These things are really worrying. The everyday task is tremendous. I have to share my love and whatever I have.

Pastoral ministry is more a caring than a preaching. In these circumstances I don't just go up to the pulpit and preach a sermon. The problems people go through affect me mentally and physically. I carry things in my diary, but I carry them also in my spirit. Most of the things stick on my heart and it takes a long time to get over them. Pastoring is caring for body, soul and spirit and it's a ministry which some parts of the church are missing out on. I believe God made people for one another and the more joy you can bring to somebody through the ministry the more you can enjoy being a minister.

16

CARING FOR THE COMMUNITY

I became involved with different types of issues to do with community because as a leader I am placed at the frontier of justice and peace. When there is injustice I am affected. I am concerned. So if I get a complaint that someone is wrongly treated in police custody or picked up and charged when they are innocent I go straight up to the police station. If I'm resented I make sure I ask for the person in charge. Most times I find the people at the head are quite sympathetic and will listen to me. On one occasion I wrote to the commander in chief and invited him to the community where he could sit and listen to local people with their grievances and hurts.

I am involved in the heart of community. My mission is not just from the pulpit to the pew. I make sure I march alongside the struggle to achieve a plural and just society. When I went to prizegiving day at the school my daughters attended I found there were no black governors in a school with 70 per cent ethnic minority children. Now I had to raise the question 'Why?' So I went straight to the head teacher. When I see some of the housing conditions of people in my borough then I go to the right agent. Somebody has to take up these issues because they affect people, and if I am leading people then that affects me too.

Most leaders of the black-led churches are taking on board social care for the community, such as adoption into black families, education, women's issues. You name it . . . awareness is really catching on. Where the mainstream churches left off from addressing themselves to the needs of different ethnic minority groups, the black-led churches are now filling the gaps and finding their rightful caring position within communities across the country, especially in the inner city where situations of deprivation and poverty exist.

The conditions that face ethnic minorities demand much more attention and concern from leaders, especially the church leaders. In recent years the black-led churches have taken on board a more positive response to social and political issues. Many projects which cater for the social, physical, mental and spiritual needs of the congregation have developed, such as work with the elderly, holiday play schemes, mother and toddler groups. There are many false beliefs from the indigenous population as to the true functions of black-led churches. They are often regarded as dogmatic in their doctrines and teaching, and likely to separate themselves from social and political activities. This is far from the truth. The black-led churches are among the most outstanding and powerful black organisations and are open to all people. They are in the communities of Britain as a tower of strength and support for people of all colours, tribes, and races. There is a direct mission of caring and love and concern. The worship is free and welcoming and conducted by ordinary lay people most times. Anyone can join in and participate. The fellowship is like an extended family. The men are called brothers, the women sisters, and the aged ones mothers, and sometimes Dad.

We try to break down the barrier between ages. Our congregation is not just old people or middle-aged but also the very young. In the club sometimes children are there sitting on one of the elderly persons' knees. It brings back those lovely memories for them because their own children have grown up. Then the teenagers and twenty- and thirty-year-olds are coming in and learning to appreciate their old people. That's a value that should not be removed from any society. Old people should be given their dignity. Back home we had to give people their title respectfully. We couldn't just pass them whistling or shouting or saying a rude word. They would tell our parents and we would be reprimanded.

In my own church's care for the elderly we run a five-day-a-week club, though it's more like a community than a club. Old people need a hot nourishing meal. That's very important. But they need friends and fellowship too. So they have their meal and they chat and play games and tell stories of the past. Sometimes they discover close relatives and neighbours from their town or village back home. They never realised before that they were in Britain. It's like jigsaw pieces coming together. They make new friends and then they have someone to talk to and telephone. They are taught about ways of coping when they are getting old in a strange country. After worship on a Sunday they have someone to eat with. In our culture Sunday is a special day. There's a special way of dressing, special way of eating. It's one of the best meals on a Sunday with friends. The doors are open in church. People are around. We eat and we chat. People stay for another session if they want, or there are kind hands around to take the elderly people home in their own time.

We have a very strong senior citizens' choir. In this country when people get old it seems they don't play the piano any more. They don't bring the flowers to church. They don't play the organ any more. Even though people are getting on in age they should not be left out. They should feel as if they are still part of things. We have a ninety-year-old in our club who knows everything that's going on. She's very lively and aware. Then there's an eighty-five-year-old who comes on the march with us and who feels to be a part of the keep fit club, and a seventy-year-old who sings the lead in the choir.

Old black people would not flock to the bingo and to the pub. One in ten old black people will be scrambling out to the pub and hanging on to a beer. They want church. It's their way of life. They want to die peacefully. I find them sometimes struggling out to the post office to draw their pension so if I see them I go up and chat. Something can be done and should be done. It's a growing concern. We find old black people abandoned in this land. Living in substandard conditions. Under-privileged. The life they are living is far below good quality. These are the people who've been keeping the buses, the underground and the hospitals running. British Railways. Building sites. Whatever. The people who came in to fight the war, or who came in the fifties. They worked. They paid tax. They helped to shape communities.

Some of the children have gone to America and Canada because things were not getting any better for them and the old people are living here, tucked away in some underprivileged kind of life. Not everyone earns enough money to buy a house in Kent or somewhere in the suburban areas. We could say all old people's problems and circumstances are alike, black or white. We hear statutory bodies saying, 'There are very few old black people around, or from the other ethnic minorities. Their families look after them.' It's because they are not prepared to face up to the growing problem of people from different cultures getting old. They are not trying to understand the cultures. They go and research, and come up with reports about the needs of minorities without consulting or listening to people from those groups. Authorities need to listen to people from ethnic minorities about how best old people can be cared for in a manner not to hasten their death.

Old black people are not finding a comfort in sheltered accommodation. It's not their culture. The prejudices that are in old people can't be changed now. Put one or two black people among sixty white and this means isolation. There is no communication, or real relationship. It makes them die quicker. Black people who come from the West Indies and Africa and other places have a home of their own. They have a piece of land. They have independence. They have something to hold on to. At the back of their minds they are going home. When they are put in a small place with a tiny bed, and items for which they have worked and achieved are taken away, it is a tragedy for them. Old people love company. They love to know that they can entertain. Old people can't even move in the sort of accommodation that is given to them. I think there should be a group home that gives old black people that sense of belonging. They need this to survive. They need to feel wanted, not dumped.

In our culture we do not move our old people out of the community. We treat them like an antique, within the family. The focus is on them for information, for instruction, for counselling. If it's a first baby, marriage, whatever, they would be the centre. They feel they are wanted and they have their integrity. They say it used to happen in this land in the past. It's the extended family that black people have lost in this country and it has affected them severely. When our people go into hospital some of the stories are very sad. They are told, 'Shut up.' Back home we wouldn't dare to speak to an elderly person like that. Black people have lost integrity and dignity here. I know things have changed, but I believe these are values worth hanging on to. Human dignity is something that is precious and valuable. We can't just throw out everything for new, else we'll throw out the baby and the bathwater.

The eldest member of our church was ninety-four when he died. When he was very ill in hospital I turned up to sit and chat with him. He had his senses. Before I entered the ward I could hear his voice. He was praying, repeating, 'The Lord is my shepherd.' He knew that his end was near but he had so much belief in God. And though the nurses made a mock of him that faith took him to the very end. I also have a Christian lady from Guyana. She's ninety-six now. When I go there she sits me down and tells me a few things about God. That's what the older generation know best and they hold on to it. They're holding on to a faith that carries them through their lives to the end. To me that's what Christianity is all about.

What a lot of people do not understand and what I would like the black youngsters born in this country to realise is that most of the people who came to this country from the Caribbean or Africa have a home, some cattle, a piece of land, faith, some security. They did not come from living in a tree as the English people thought. It's a myth. Even if I didn't have a house in Jamaica I could pick up all my family and go back and there would be sufficient houses for us to live in. My father's, my brother's, my sister's in-laws. It's not like Britain. If you're homeless God help you.

The people who are suffering are the ones who haven't got the means to go back. Their mind is already bent toward the system here. Most of the people who suffer these levels of deprivation, especially in the inner cities, do not know the system. They cannot fight it. It breaks them. A lot of the breakdown in black people is because of how they have been treated. They have lived here for a long time but found no home, no acceptance. They have suffered homelessness, broken-up families, loneliness and depression. I know one lady who I am counselling now. Her children are in care, one without proper reason. She lives in very substandard accommodation in a little bedsitter. Recently they took away her pension book so she was left without money for weeks. She just keeps crying, crying, crying. I know the next thing is going to be a mental breakdown. Though we intercede we cannot get any proper answers. These are circumstances which drive people to breaking point. If a lady was like that back in the Caribbean there is no way that neighbours would let her suffer for food or for a proper place to live.

We have just bought a five-bedroomed house because

of the homelessness in our congregation. We are able to house five or six youngsters. All that is part of what people now want to see when they ask what the black-led churches are doing for the social needs. There is an awareness running through all the black-led churches that the gospel applies to the whole person. I knew days when my children were cared for so lovingly by sisters in the church and many other times when I myself was short of food. Without my even telling the leader some instinct let the brothers and sisters know we had a need.

When it was evident that some people weren't getting any jobs we bought newspapers and helped. There is not a great deal of unemployment within the congregations of the black-led churches. If someone knew that a person didn't have a job they would begin looking out for them. But I know for a fact black people don't get certain jobs. I have researched it. There are many black people in this country doing a job far below their qualifications or not getting promoted.

The unemployment situation is going to get worse and I am very concerned. Unemployment among black people, especially the younger ones, will be the reason why they will be picked upon as muggers and criminals. Some media specialise in bringing out reports on crime areas to let it look as if it's the black people doing all the crime. I am very scared if these issues are not handled with wisdom. It gives people the wrong impression.

Every aspect of achieving anything towards success on the part of black people in this country has got to be a political fight. And I don't mean an easy one either. There is always a reason why it can't happen. Changes are not freely and willingly happening for black communities in this country. So the people who haven't got the guts and the courage to fight give up. There's an empty school in our borough we are negotiating with the council to use as a Caribbean centre. We've been fighting to achieve a Caribbean centre in the area for more than five years now. The black community is growing and we need somewhere people can identify themselves; a place where they can go for information, which will take on board children, deal with the community positively. So up comes this school. We've had several meetings. We've held campaigns. We've spoken to the leader of the council. We've gone to all kinds of sources. But we've never seen anything come of it. So we're sunk down in despair again. After years of negotiation there is still no certainty about achieving it.

When we are very soft and quiet and tackle the issues academically the way white people want us to do then possibly we have more sympathisers. When we are firm and pushy and say it in an angry tone of voice then we are criticised that we are too strong. We are torn between two attitudes in the way people respond to us. I want to play the game because I want to see changes. But if it means that I have to speak out from my gut level, how I feel, and let the anger come out before changes come then I will. I am not afraid to let people see the feelings that are buried there. Possibly most times I get no sympathisers but I've got the strength of the church.

What makes me feel justified is because on my patch, at grass roots level, things are happening. I not only speak as a voice for the people, I actually do things. Elderly people know how to pick up the phone and call. We've set up projects. Young people can be identified with something positive that is going on. Broken-up families can get strength. There is a system that works. Local authorities may give grants to help get these projects off the ground but it's all a part of their own duties we have taken on board that they are helping us to fulfil.

17

BROTHERS AND SISTERS IN CHRIST?

There are people who understand the whole issue of racism, people who want to go back to their different communities and promote the work we are doing. But how do we get racist people to listen to what is hurting their neighbours, to see what is not good practice within a community? The media could help, but they don't. All they want to promote is the muggings. I would say it's a constant fight. As long as I'm on the scene it's going to remain an issue because a community can only be the kind of community that the people make it to be. It doesn't matter what subject is taken on board, or researched to see how to promote good practice, racism comes into it. There's a measure of racism involved in women's issues, housing, and unemployment. It's sad. Look at the issues in South Africa. In the face of God how could human beings degrade another human being like they do?

In a sense I see apartheid in this country. Not as open as South Africa but similar in the way we are treated like an outsider as a black person and denied our rights. I still don't feel at home in England after thirty years. The way black people are talked about on the media, or the way an issue can be dragged out to make it look as though it has never happened before in this country when someone black is an offender. The slogans we read from day to day. 'Go home' and all that. White people from South Africa are allowed in. No hassle. We, from a former British colony, they disown and reject.

My great disappointment is we are fighting these laws on every hand but we seem to get nowhere in the end. Or those people who represent us in government have no sympathy towards the way we feel about it. The National Front still marches under the British flag. Nothing drastic has been done by leaders and people in power to wipe out racism. Britain is not really changing with any significant speed. The process to achieve peace and justice and to work towards a plural society is moving too slowly.

I went out to look for a birthday card for a little girl and all the birthday cards on the stall showed little white children. Not that I am prejudiced against white children but how can I buy a picture of a white girl to give to my black child? We need to see more positive images of black people in this country. It will take black and white people together to help to wipe out racism in Britain. The problem of racism is not with the black people, it is with the white people. The manifestation of the act of racism is in institutions and organisations, so those who are affected by it are the powerless. As long as I live in Britain I will have to champion the cause of right and wrong, of peace and justice. Every person has a right to feel that they are human and they have a right to live as equals. Some of us who are really committed to a gospel of justice and peace can't be quiet on these issues. They stare us in the face.

Racism affects every part of our society, every institution, including the Church. Invariably it has been swept under the carpet but it can't be any longer. The people who do not want to tackle it are the people who are making it bad, those who are not accepting their own racism. They shift it all the time. When racism is under discussion they begin to talk about something else. I said to somebody, 'How would you feel if my son, my black David, wanted to marry your white daughter?' The emotion, the look, the changing of the colour told me how people are not genuine in coming to terms with their racism.

I'm not saying it's easy. All those years of education have set up white people to consider themselves better than black people. But if folks look across the table at me and say, 'You black so and so,' if I'm not accepted because of the colour of my skin, that doesn't mean that something is wrong with me. The wrong comes when individuals and organisations discriminate against me.

The question I want to ask is, 'Why is it so hard for Christians to speak out openly on the issue of racism?' The Church has not really put into action this whole issue of Jesus' own teaching, 'Love your neighbour as yourself.' This is one of the most difficult battles for me. I can accept what is coming from secular organisations and secular people but cannot accept the sort of wolf in sheep's clothing attitude from Christians in this country. They say, 'I love you. I love you', but their heart is not in their words. They are very charitable, but the love of God is deeper than material gifts. This is where the Church fails. They have preached the gospel to many people outside this land but when you come back here it's something different. What made me change from being a Baptist to a Pentecostal was the experience of rejection I found in British churches. You might say, 'Well, that was 1957/58,' but recently I preached at a church and stood there to shake hands afterwards and people just turned their heads away. I'm sure this is something God will condemn. How can we love God and hate our brothers?

The Christianity I know and accept is a Christianity which affects my life around the clock. It's gut conscious that once I'm a Christian I'm changed. I can't accept the kind of Christianity that only affects people on Sunday. The tradition that people go and sing liturgies and songs and for the rest of the week can afford to be prejudiced against somebody else can no longer be tolerated. It's the culture of selfishness, individualism. People think of themselves and not others.

There are real obstacles which are stopping the blessings of God upon Christians in this country. They are self-made barriers which have gone up. Black/white, female/male, differences in denomination/different ways of worshipping. These things keep us divided. We should listen to what our Lord Jesus Christ has to say. We should listen to the plea in his prayer as he reached out to his father and asked that we might be one. We should look at the barriers that divide us and work to break them down. I am a Pentecostal but my approach to worship does not stop me from sharing love and fellowship with Christians from other denominations. In fact this gives me an opportunity for learning.

There have been years of misunderstanding of the black-led churches. They were there on the doorstep of the indigenous churches for over three decades and no one seemed to take any notice. They were ignored and pushed aside and rejected. In the white-led churches

135

ministry is seen as coming from Oxford and Cambridge and other theological colleges. In some of the black-led churches there is no set pattern of leadership training, though it has begun to happen in recent years. We have seen the need for theology, the need for teaching and training. Overstone in Northampton is one of the largest black colleges. It takes on board diplomas and degrees and has its own teaching staff. The Institute of Christian Training provides theological education for the New Testament Assembly. Students come to lectures on a weekly basis and the certificates and degrees are validated by St. David's University in Lampeter. There are many other theological institutes within the black-led churches. Most of our pastors are trained in Sunday School work and in theological subjects both here and in America, though we still do not believe that to preach the gospel you must go to college.

Looking back we could say that the black-led churches have come out of the valley and have found their way alongside the mainstream churches. We are equal partners in ministry, in mission and in the work of the kingdom, yet black Christians are not encouraged by their white counterparts. Participation is not consistent. Sometimes there is a one-off event in which we have joint worship. One World Week, the Week of Prayer for Christian Unity, the Women's World Day of Prayer. When committees are set up across the country and plans for evangelism are being discussed the black church is invited as an afterthought. They do not look to the black Christians as if they can learn from them in the way of missions and evangelism. Sometimes if they do get asked on committees it is just a token black face. It is not equal participation. When we go there and put proposals together they don't accept what we say. But if somebody white says a similar thing it's taken on board. I have had that experience personally till I became fed up with these all white committees.

Nowadays most mainstream churches have got black people participating in the congregation, although there are not many black leaders in the white churches. In some churches ninety per cent of the people are black but the leaders are white. Some of the most outstanding traditions within the white churches are not training black people to be priests and ministers. This is still to come. We have recently experienced the first black bishop in the Anglican tradition. This should have happened years ago. We are not experiencing the Roman Catholics making their black people priests unless one comes from overseas. If we look in the theological colleges we will not find many black people. This is an area that the Church needs to look at with concern. Changes are needed now for the sake of the younger generation. We must provide role models in all areas of institutions in this country.

Secular organisations are adapting. Why is theChurch not tackling the issue? Throughout the fifties, sixties, even seventies we couldn't buy ethnic minority foods like hot pepper sauce, red kidney beans, sweet potato, or mangoes in Sainsbury's or Tesco's or even the market. Yet most of the things we cherish we find in these places today. Because communities are multi-cultural, consideration is taken to cater for the needs of the people. The Church should be at the forefront of a similar process. But what does the Church do? They sit upon their thrones. Jesus says, 'Go into all the world and bring the good news to all the nations, people and tongues.' They sit there and say, 'Come.'

Most of the attitudes in the Church have not changed since the early fifties. The whole Western theology sways the religious part of life. I no more want to listen to Western theology. It has a whole lot of falsehood. A lot of black people have lost faith in European Christianity. The blue-eyed, blonde Jesus and all that. Christianity should be taken seriously. As I look at Christians in this country I see each denomination having a certain belief and a certain direction. They each stick to their own traditions and few are open for renewal, for learning, for sharing, or for the work of the Holy Spirit.

Britain is blessed with various cultures and with many Christians from different backgrounds and traditions. For Christians to genuinely come together in this country should not be so difficult. Many people are working at every level so that the Spirit can move in the direction of bringing people together. As Jesus rightly said, the world will only know that we are Christians when we love one another. For us to see signs of hope will be to see young and old, women and men, black and white being free to worship together, to share their love for God, and to learn from one another. Barriers and bondages can bring pain and for most church people the frustration of not being free is causing a lot of hurt. Being hung up on tradition is causing a lot of people to lose their way, especially the young. They know there is a God but because Christianity is put in so many different packages they are asking questions. I believe that when the Church unites, when Christians of different colour, creed and skin begin to preach the gospel together, to share and worship together, then there will be a genuine reformation of the Spirit in this land.

18

BRIDGE-BUILDING

A lot of hurt has been generated over the years because of rejection by white Christians and the way black people have been treated. The scars are still there. Better understandings have been developed among the churches these days, both black and white, but there are still areas that need healing. Christians need to reconcile their differences at this present time by meeting, and developing relationships in a spirit of forgiveness.

I know that many of our black Christians will not go out to white people because they have been on the receiving end for too long. Nevertheless black Christians must not take the past to determine today or tomorrow. Now is the time for healing and reconciliation. It will have to be a two-way effort. Black and white together. The whole issue of genuine Christian fellowship and love needs to be taken more seriously. It's bridge-building time. When we cross the bridge we must not cross as strangers, we must cross as friends.

This is why I was involved with Zebra, a Christian-based race relation group, that takes on board breaking down barriers. Over the years Zebra has brought various groups together to talk out things and build relationships across races, cultures and peoples. I was on the committee long before I took a job with them. There is great satisfaction in meeting people face to face and talking with them. If I receive a letter inviting me to an event I see the letter but I don't see the organiser's face. I don't know what attitude they display towards race. But when they shake my hand and smile with me, and say 'Come over' and I can look them in the eye, this means something. I begin to realise the type of person they are and what they are saying to me can be understood quite clearly.

There's a lot of myth and misunderstanding on the part of white people when it comes to race. Among Christians as well. It's a fact that Britain is now multi-racial, multi-faith, multi-cultural. It's bound to remain with us. There's another population of black people coming up. This is something we should be looking at more closely. Race issues must not be pushed under the carpet. Some white people are doing their best to champion the cause of justice on the part of black people but I'm afraid they've got to do it so that we can feel it. I've got something to contribute, they've got something to contribute, but when we are working together then it's far more meaningful. It's not 'Come. Let me do it for you.' It should not be them making a policy or approaching what they think is a right strategy. It's us together building trust and confidence in each other. Speak to us before laying down policies or setting up a committee. Ask, 'What do you think we should do?' See if we have a suggestion. We do not want to go ahead fighting a cause out of hate and dislike for one another. We want to fight it with love. We must challenge, champion, campaign, make decisions together. I feel that's the only way we are going to win.

I'm always saying across conferences and to individuals that we do not admire people who set up organisations and promote committees to fight for black people. I do not want the white person to fight for me. I appreciate it most when we are fighting together. Agencies that deliver services have a marvellous way of setting up committees and panels and issuing reports about the needs of black people without involving black people themselves. It's the way things have been approached over the years. White people need to understand we do appreciate what's going on, but we want to be a part of it. We do not admire the good, patronising, stereotyping approach. Why not let us do things together? Often there are no items on the agenda to do with the issues facing the black community or to take on board the sort of things we are doing in our own community to promote good practice. All the discussions are going in the other direction.

The churches are like that as well. Instead of coming to talk they think they have the answer. When they are having conferences or big celebrations like Greenbelt they never think there are established black people in this country who are good speakers. It amuses me sometimes to see how they make a fuss of the black people from abroad, from America, and other countries, but they don't treat black people here with the same respect and recognition. It's as though they are thinking, 'Well . . . I don't have to put up with this one for much longer. They're here and out of sight again.' There are black speakers in Britain who can draw hundreds of followers but such leaders are overlooked. It is very bad if people who are living and serving here cannot be recognised.

Some organisers and promoters are beginning to realise this but quite a lot more needs to be done.

There are some encouraging signs. Far more people are coming together now than they were even five years ago. There have been areas in the white highlands for instance, where they have never heard of the black-led churches. They never had any kind of relationship. Yet now we are sharing services, sharing communion. The British Council of Churches within its various departments has stretched out its hand in fellowship to many of the black-led churches. The New Testament Assembly has recently become a member church of the BCC. The Lent courses organised by the churches have brought black and white Christians together in a new way. People who went to church in the same locality, sometimes down the road, but had never met, came together for the first time. This is my hope for the Church. To see all of God's children come to some closer understanding and be able to share each other's cultures. Worship together, pray together, challenge racism together. As a priority.

For a long time we could almost call the black-led churches the hidden church because although we were there in the community we were largely ignored by the indigenous churches. There were no real, genuine relationships. Only tenant and landlord. Now thankfully networks across the denominations like the Evangelical Alliance, the Evangelical Coalition for Urban Mission, Zebra Project, the Catholic Association for Racial Justice, the inter-church process, 'Not Strangers but Pilgrims', have developed links and are doing a remarkable work in breaking down barriers and building bridges across the gaps between Christians. We don't have to

143

accept each other's styles but we can worship together and fellowship together and that's important. That's the way we are going to begin to accept each other. These are precious signs of hope which are developing. I trust that in the future there will be similar events that can enhance existing networks to draw all of God's people together in fellowship and unity. Until we can share our faith, our love, share each other's weaknesses and strengths, we will not be fulfilling the whole gospel Jesus Christ has preached. We need our journeyings to be together for the future. Christians everywhere, whether they are black or white, must forget their denominational barriers and begin to create one large umbrella that all of God's people can be seen sheltering under together, sharing their common humanity.

19

A PROPHETIC VOICE

I left Zebra in 1983 and ended up working for Nathan Institute, taking on board training and consultation for racial justice. The organisation originated from the Church and most of the work we do is tuned to the Church. I strongly believe that the Church has to be an example. It's very important for places such as colleges that are training men for ministry to know something about the multi-racial community and the way to treat and understand people from other cultures.

It needs black and white to raise the whole question of racism and deal with it properly though it hurts to really share some of the things with white groups. They twist it out of context and put it their own way. Most white people don't have the patience to go through some of the exercises about accepting their own racism. It's very few who can do that. Someone did share a story with me about how he stood at a bus stop and a Rolls Royce pulled up with a white chauffeur. Seated in the passenger seats at the back were two black men. Straightaway he said, 'It should be the other way round.' He didn't realise how racist he was until he stopped to consider why he reacted like that. Not many white people will admit those sort of things.

On several occasions I've wished some white people would put on a black skin just for a minute and go on the streets. Then they would realise. Sometimes I don't know what to do to get the story home. It is essential to do something positive about educating people. It's not sufficient to have friends of a different colour and to eat together, and share things in common. It needs an inward acceptance that regardless of the colour of my skin I am on the same level as you. Equal. I can do the job you do. I'm able to conduct myself in the manner in which you conduct yourself.

The Conference for Christian Partnership is unique in bringing people together in a positive way. It is a project that takes on both spiritual and social issues and brings together ordained people like bishops, vicars and pastors with lay representatives from all kinds of traditions; black and white. We meet four times a year and build bridges across the many difficulties and problems that there are. We have worship celebrations, spend weekends together, and challenge things like immigration laws and policing. We do not only talk them through at conference but send letters far and wide raising questions to do with injustices.

'Faith in the City', the report the Archbishop of Canterbury commissioned, has been a very good and valuable document in relation to the whole ecumenical field. It has been a long time coming but it has come in time. It has highlighted the religious system, drawn attention to issues which have been ignored over the years, and shown the poverty of the Church's response. 'Faith in the City' has motivated and inspired a lot of well-thinking people within the churches in this country. I am hoping that in the months ahead, whatever this report

146

has uncovered we will see some positive results coming out. It has meant such a lot to people like ourselves who are working at grass roots level and are struggling without any proper resources. So often we have no proper buildings, and no proper funding to evangelise and care for the needs of people in the community, especially within the inner cities.

The Church is living in evil days. It is a time when unity is going to be our strength. We have to work together in order to combat the evils of these times. Issues of peace, justice, racism and war are universal problems which concern us. We must tackle them together if we are to overcome them. It is important that the churches be agents for peace and justice in the world.

It's about time we looked across the barriers of colour and denomination and got together as Christians. Christianity is moving from beneath the feet of people in this country. There is a tendency of a great force that is fighting the faith. Christians cannot afford to fight against one another when there are so many forces fighting against us. We cannot be complacent at this present time. If we are we will be trampled spiritually. John Wesley wouldn't allow this. William Carey wouldn't allow this. Livingstone wouldn't allow this. None of those missionaries who fought and lost their limbs for the faith would want to see a limbless Church.

Even if people don't respect the black-led churches that have sprung up in this country because of the way we worship, or because we're black, they've got to respect us for the gospel which has spread and reached so many people. When I arrived here thirty years ago there were not many black-led churches. Just one or two. Now we have over 120,000 worshipping Christians

147

in the black-led churches in Britain. With these thousands comes the prayer, the preaching, the mission. Many church buildings that would have become warehouses or supermarkets, or been knocked down, have been bought by these newer churches and the worship and the witness of God still rings out from them. Many people's lives have been changed. A lot of churches in our borough are coming together to hold an open air event on one of the estates that has been vandalised and run down. There's a vast array of concrete buildings and high rise flats with many families cut off. A lot of needs. We must reach the people with the gospel. When it comes to humanity the Church has a message all the year round. The gospel addresses itself to every situation.

We need to march with the sort of evangelism that would value the message of Jesus Christ to this country. Let secularism take its course but the Church should not water down the values or the message of Jesus himself. There is a cowardice amongst Christians. They are frightened to offend. I think Christians should speak out on subjects like abortion, racism, apartheid, the immigration laws; issues that affect their brothers and sisters. The Church has the dynamics and the influence to speak out but they don't.

It is the Church that should be speaking for the poor. 'What does the Lord require of you?' the prophet says, 'But to do justly and to love mercy.' The Church is doing what it can, but it is not its best. As Christians we need to deal our bread to the hungry. That's a command. It's not doing a favour to a poor person to love and feed them. Jesus said we are to love. Christians have to speak for the poor and we have to do it together. And that's far from where we are at the moment.

There are signs. A small minority. The kind of hope I am looking forward to is that people within the Christian context who have the influence and the power should speak out on those issues that spoil good practice. There are some people who are not in a position to speak, and we have got to be their voice. It's a whole question of power and powerlessness. You can put a question sign saying 'Who are the powerless?' but once you begin to touch areas like these you are accused of getting very political. How often do the press and media say, 'Leave it alone' when the bishops touch on such issues. We can't. We have to fight and work from where we are in the different communities. Though people don't come to church they are still God's people.

We don't use the pulpit to preach politics as a subject but the person who is going to be in leadership, in charge of people, like a pastor or bishop, of course they are involved in politics. They have to look after their congregation physically as well as spiritually. I don't take it seriously when the media say the preachers must leave politics and attend to their congregation. The Bible is political. The story of Moses and all that. God has something to say about injustices. Jesus was political. We live in a political world. Better that the clergy and people who preach the gospel are aware of the system of politics.

Some of the churches have a whole lot to blame for what goes on in South Africa, especially the Dutch Christians and English Christians. Yet the churches have not really come out to do something positive. Even to put pressure on the government to bring about sanctions. It's all talk, writing and books. Some of us get very frustrated. I want to see people take a leading action. I want to shout it from the mountaintop. Free

South Africa from apartheid. Help to fight racism in Britain. People are equals. We are all God's creation.

I believe that this country has a lot of power and influence. It needs to use such power more positively in helping to denounce laws that cause suffering to humanity. Whatever attitude Britain displays is an example for other nations. It is known to the rest of the world as a Christian country. The first Bible I owned came from Cambridge in England and was called the King James' version. It taught me that one of the greatest commandments is to love my neighbour. Christianity went from this country to all the world. What about Christianity here on our doorstep?

20

A CONTINUING BATTLE

I know it is the Holy Spirit that breaks down the pride in me. Arrogance, anger and those things that are contrary to my Christian conviction. I couldn't do that kind of work myself. It's one of the hardest, most difficult jobs to work on yourself. It's like a dressmaker who never spends time to make up a dress for herself. Or a builder building the most beautiful house but not for his own use. If you're a tradesperson you always leave yourself till last. There are times when I come across things in my own experience I cannot do anything about. I dare not touch it. I just have to say, 'Lord, it's over to you.'

I've found this a great help in the ministry. I couldn't do half the things in my own strength. I can't speak sometimes. I just have to pray and leave it there. Even when I am not preaching, when I am faced with various temptations or cast down with social cares and pressures, the Holy Spirit is standing there. I can actually feel that someone is with me. The strength I receive inwardly couldn't be my own making. It takes that power of the Holy Spirit to help me to be what I am.

If somebody hurts and upsets me and I say, 'OK. That's it, I'm going to take my revenge,' straightaway I can hear the Holy Spirit speaking to me. I can read the very tone. It doesn't only affect my hearing, it changes my heart as well. Instead of meeting the person and being very rash and angry I begin to come out with the spirit of love. Even in our own experience as a family there are some things we do better not to touch in case they explode. Somebody may say, 'Count to ten,' but I sing a little song or say a prayer and leave it to cool. I never dreamed I could tell God the things that I tell him. When I come back to them I always find an answer.

Not long ago my husband was very ill. When the doctors told me the condition I knew it was going to be difficult. It's best to be honest and have no secrets but I still wondered, 'Is it wise to tell?' My assurance all the time was that the Holy Spirit was going to attend to that condition and surely he did. He has always been a constant help and strength.

Twice I have faced serious illness and the prayer of faith has healed the condition. Once from an internal ulcer and once from asthma. The ulcer was so bad I thought I was going to die. I even talked it over seriously with my husband and told him what to do when I went. I remember clearly how I then fell into a deep sleep, deeper than an ordinary sleep. During the sleep I prayed that the Lord would heal me or take me home by death. When I came back from the sleep I could hear those in the room praying and could immediately feel the relief of the pain. The following day I was able to be out of bed. I went straight away to pray for someone else who was very sick and she too was healed. I've struggled through a lot of illness. I've been in hospital three times for major surgery and had it not been for divine intervention I might not have lived.

Since I became a committed Christian I have no fear

of facing the day of death. For me it's not 'Good night' but 'Good morning.' I heard a story from the West Indies about a young couple. They had just arrived home from church where the husband had been preaching the sermon. He was lying down on the verandah while the young wife was cooking the dinner. He was talking to her as she worked and asked, 'If you had fruit on a tree, ripe and ready to eat, would you cut it down, or leave it to rot, for the birds to eat?' I don't know if he was trying to warn her, or if it was a parable given by God, but he died that evening. She was only young with her first baby. That hurt. She couldn't get over it.

I don't know why my mother died at such a young age. It led to a lot of questions. I couldn't get over that. She made us one of the loveliest suppers that evening. I read the Bible at her bedside that night. Psalm 94. She kissed me at 9 p.m. Hours later she lay dead. I carried the hurt for five years. I've come to accept it now because none of us can live in this world for ever. Sometime or other we have to go, regardless of the hurt it leaves behind, but it took me a long time to come to terms with my hurt. I still can't visit my mother's grave. I can sympathise with young people, children who have lost a mother, the people I know who suffer bereavement.

I preach from that psalm my mother loved, Psalm 94, many times. She loved God as being a righteous and just God and that whatever happened God would do justice in the end. When I look at the injustices in the world I read this psalm and get such encouragement. It's all tied up. The puzzle is coming back. I was questioned, 'Why Psalm 94 when so many love Psalm 23?' Many people in the Caribbean will read Psalm 23 for all occasions. They'll read it when a child is born. Even place it in the baby's cot. It's read at morning and it's read at night. People rely on the word of God. They feel that God is there. Though they don't see him he's there in their homes, and wherever. They would call on the word of God and feel it would influence any other spirits that were around. So I would have expected my mother to take Psalm 23 instead. But with Psalm 94 I can see what she was up against. Injustices. Things I did not understand. It's coming back together and has given me great courage and strength.

My deep belief in God is derived from my home background. I have respect and gratitude for the way my father laid down a strict religious upbringing for the entire family. Time was set aside for prayer and Bible study, but it was not only preached, it was lived out in my own home. It has always been a home where there was warmth and welcome. For children, teenagers, adults, the entire community. We were taught by our father to love everybody. Now my eldest brother is a bishop, the next to him is rooted in the faith, my eldest sister is a minister. We are not followers of the Baptist religion which we grew up in but we can appreciate the grounding one hundred per cent. Most of us carry that foundation faith along with us. Today I can draw on those rich and meaningful patterns. I have seen a reason for my coming to this country. I know exactly what God is doing with my life. I want to stay here yet a little while. There is a ministry here for me which I want to fulfil. I could look back over the thirty years and throw my hands in the sky and say, 'Thank God that I did come to Britain.' My dreams have been shattered in a sense but I have learned a lot. I'm not saying if I hadn't come here I wouldn't be educated because I had the chance of further education in Jamaica. And I don't say if I hadn't come here I wouldn't have married. Surely I would. My benefits are that I'm able to choose between two cultures. There's a lot of good in my coming to Britain. And I would fail to say the truth if I didn't say that. At the same time I have a lot of regrets. It's been hard going. If God hadn't carried me through those struggles I would certainly have given up.

I don't have to be in East London at all. I could move out. Possibly go back to my own country. I don't have to do the work I do. If it was for my own self I possibly wouldn't be in this country now. But deep in my heart I am touched. I want to do something about the situation. There are people around that I can't afford to walk out on. I want to be in the struggle. I don't just mean for black people. Every human being has a right to be of value. Black and white. When laws and oppression stand in the way it can be hurtful. People don't understand half the story. For those people who are really and truly getting their hands dirty most of the time they are pushing against pressure and frustration. It's like a competition. It's no use saying, 'People must help themselves.' Sometimes they need help to do that. When I look back at the years that I have been working, and where I have reached, in a sense it's encouraging but there's a lot more that can be done.

I've been on television several times. I did an hour-long documentary three or four years ago which highlighted the church's community work and the social activities and everything. Then the Zebra programme was on for three quarters of an hour about the value of black and white people talking over our misunderstandings face to face. Recently I was interviewed because I had invited the Archbishop of Canterbury to one of our services and we were talking about unity and part of the service was shown. I've been on Goodnight, Thought for the Day, TV AM when they launched a religious section, and quite a few other appearances. It doesn't bother me. The only thing is, sometimes when I have to appear on television I go out the next day, and walk in a shop people may say, 'Look', with excitement.

Thank God there is a little change in this country but there's still a long way to go. I want to encourage black people to stand up and be counted for the skills they have to offer society. We have brought a lot of good practice to communities in this country. A lot of caring. I have learned to appreciate whatever I had from a child though I do not want to hold on to the tradition where men took women for granted.

I'm not a captive to a house. I don't want to be called a housewife. I'm not married to a house. I'm married to a man who knows that we are two free people. I'm not fighting to be free. I am free. We order our home and live together in peace and share whatever there is. I'm not a captive in the church. I'm liberated to work alongside a man within the ministry and I feel liberated inside. I cannot repeat often enough that we, as women, have got to claim our liberation and that the Church should realise that the gospel has liberated us all; both men and women. I have no hang-ups about being black. If you think something is wrong with me because I'm black that proves it's not me who has it wrong. What I've seen on the front of the race issue in this country is that things are not moving fast enough, as they ought to move. After so much work has been put in over the past decade. Some stories are sad to hear when so much effort has been put in.

I wouldn't say the situation is deteriorating but we can achieve a lot more if people don't get discouraged and we continue the trend. I never dreamed there would be a black guard at Buckingham Palace in 1988. Or the first black bishop in the Anglican Church. People think it's a major breakthrough but it's too slow. This should have been happening long ago. It's just a way marker. Telling people what should be done. We have to really fight for these things to happen when conscious and intelligent people ought to know without being told. It's embarrassing when we have to put pressure one. People think we are rebels. The sort of areas they are willing to do something about now, if there hadn't been a riot they wouldn't have bothered. I can see the prophecy of Enoch Powell about the bloodbath in Britain coming true if we are not conscious of what's happening. Just as how these things happened in Brixton and other target areas, it will happen in other places. This is a message I want white people to hear. It is a battle and it will be a battle of blood but something can be done to avoid it. We should be caring now what's going to happen to the young people. The younger generation are not taking it and that's going to cause problems.

I don't think the fight is nearly finished. It's a long fight. America has fought for years and years. Black and white. Equality. Recognition. The race issue is on the front line of Britain right now. It's going to be harder than America because people are not accepting that it is an issue. It's not treated with enough concern. The Immigration and Nationality Bill was not treated with importance at all by the government or by people who

157

would be concerned and campaign for something like the Abortion Bill. There are a few pressure groups here and there working on it, but it has not been lobbied with nearly enough concern. Some people will not touch the race issue. They make very negative comments as if it's counter-productive to talk about it. There's so much stereotyping, patronising going on. The myth is that black people will disappear from Britain by tightening the immigration laws. Black people have been in this country for 450 years, whether people know their history or not. It's a long road, but at least we are on the road, and that's important. For some of us we've got to stay on the road and we've got to struggle and we've got to fight. I would like to hear more and more voice given to black people who are working towards change. It would mean less hassle, less grievances in communities, less misunderstanding and tension. It would mean that people living in suburban areas would see black people from a different eye. There have got to be changes. The whole education in this country teaches a racism that is very subtle. If it doesn't change then it's going to get like South Africa. This is why some of us have got to keep on telling the message loud and clear because we are at the receiving end.

I don't want professional black people who feel that they've got a good job now and are settled in a comfortable position in the white areas to get away with the myth that they are OK, that it's all right for black people. It is not all right, and it can't be until the system has been changed. Some people will never get where they have got. We expect them to be a voice for black people. I could have opted out but I want to be a part of the struggle and whatever it takes, whether to carry a banner or campaign in any way, at grass roots or national level, I'm prepared to do my little bit. I don't feel ready to give up. In fact I feel I should carry with me younger people and inspire those who will carry on after I am gone. We have to teach them why we are fighting this battle. It's not for me, not even for my children so much, but for my grandchildren: Crystal, Elisha and Elizabeth. It's for other people's grand-children too, the future generations that will live in this country. We've got to groove a path for them. What we do today is going to determine the future for these younger generations.

Positive things are happening. It can be done. On the international front we are going to launch a campaign for black women to join together. I will be setting up a series of prayer breakfasts to raise funds to help disad-vantaged black women. For this reason I will go to America, Canada, Africa and the Caribbean to speak to the black women in the churches about starting an organisation. I have confidence in the success of this venture. It is a vision that must be shared. This is one of the big tasks ahead of me. In my local church the next venture is to work on providing homes for homeless young people. There are lots more battles and a long, long way to go.

We have to be wise in the way we fight the battles, not to fight with violence. My children would not fight the battle the way I am fighting it; out of a Christian love, turning the cheek and so forth. This is not easily done. For me it was not easy. It's still not easy. We have had young people responding to Christianity and this is going to be a hard battle for them to learn. Whatever we do, however we fight, we should fight in the name of Jesus. I'm sure that God has got to win. When his love is within a heart it makes a difference. That's where the victory is going to be.